This story is dedicated to

Gill, my sister,

Who was there at the start of the journey,

And

To Simon, my husband,

Who will be there at its end.

"Oh, I am fortune's fool!"

William Shakespeare, *'Romeo and Juliet'*.

"But, he thought, I keep them with precision. Only I have no luck anymore. But who knows? Maybe today. Every day is a new day. It is better to be lucky. But I would rather be exact. Then when luck comes you are ready."

Ernest Hemingway, *'The Old Man and the Sea'*.

"Are you what is called a lucky man? Well, you are sad every day. Each day has its great grief or its little care. Yesterday you were trembling for the health of one who is dear to you, today you fear for your own; tomorrow it will be an anxiety about money, the next day the slanders of a calumniator, the day after the misfortune of a friend; then the weather, then something broken or lost, then a pleasure for which you are reproached by your conscience or your vertebral column; another time, the course of public affairs. Not to mention heartaches. And so on. One cloud is dissipated, another gathers. Hardly one day in a hundred of unbroken joy and sunshine. And you are of that small number who are lucky!"

Victor Hugo, *'Les Misérables'*.

"You own everything that happened to you.

Tell your stories.

If people wanted you to write warmly about them,

they should've behaved better."

Anne Lamott.

2.

Mr Lucky

Comes

To Grief.

Mr. Lucky!

Mr. Lucky? Is that a good title, a good reflection of what is contained herein? I think so, though it might not appear so at times.

This is my autobiography, my life thus far.....

There's lots of swearing and shagging to keep you entertained, lots of sorrow – no 'memoir' would be complete without yer actual sorrow....but my life has been pretty funny too so I have included some stuff to make you smile.

Everything here is the truth, the whole truth and nothing but the truth. Or at least as far as I remember it. Half a century – a lot to remember! Some things – tunes, places, voices and conversations are all so clear in my mind even now, easy to recall, yet I can't remember my mobile number half the time!

All the people are real, everything described, happened. All true.

All seen from my point of view.

I want to leave something – I can't paint, draw, write novels, invent stuff so this will have to suffice. Maybe it will end up on someone's bookshelf, passed around to friends – in that case, I WILL have left something and that will suffice. It will be good to know as I am scattered – in the land that, in my heart I never left, in all my wanderings: Kernow, back to the wild, wild sea.

Enjoy.

N.B.

P.S. MUM: Sorry for swearing. No Celestial Golden Ear Whizzes, please

P.P.S. I have referenced songs at the start of each chapter.....look them up, and see how they interpret what follows......if you want. It's a kind of interactive thing.....

Please yourself. See if I care.

CHAPTER ONE.

DOWN THE RABBITHOLE AND INTO WONDERLAND.

In which our hero discovers a home from home, more than what's good for him and falls deeply in lust.

'Together We Are Beautiful'

by Fern Kinney. No.14. April 1980.

We were beautiful! It was 'the chemistry' – or I thought it was……

~ ~ ~

Ah, what a price to pay. Getting here had been a pile of shit, a path littered with broken hearts and bad decisions and I still really had no idea about how to 'be'. I thought it was all going to be so easy:

"COOO-EEEE! EVERYONE!!! I'm gay and everyone is going to like me and not mind and I'll live happily ever after. Who's in?"

Hadn't quite turned out like that, so far. At least I didn't have syphilis; that's something.

After a (successfully passed) probationary year, I decided to look for promotion and a job in the oh-so-right-on Newham, the borough I was now living in, came up, teaching Traveller's children. It was a Scale Two post, more money, and considerably nearer home. I got the job and the end of term soon came and I left Dotheboys Hall and the fragrant Melody Winehouse and set off for pastures new.

I'd been living with Chris at Wingfield Rd. for a while now and the thought of not having to make the trip to Liverpool St. and then up to Enfield, with all its associated memories, was mightily appealing.

Right-On Newham had constructed a purpose built unit, for Travellers, on their site in Stratford, the premise being that if they wouldn't go to school, school could go to them and they employed me and A.N Other to teach them. Fully equipped and staffed, by two, we awaited the start of the Summer Term with anticipation. It was all very experimental and in September we were to have devised a curriculum for the next (and successive) school year, using the experience we were to get during that first term.

As you can imagine, dear reader, this was doomed from the outset, but money was being chucked at it by the LEA and my new salary was good plus I had no travel costs. A few pikeys to teach, a quick walk home and freedom to do what I wanted. Cornwall and my family were far away; nobody to spy or tell tales, which is just as well as there *were* tales to be told....

School began that April, and we were ready – lesson planned up to the gills, reading books chosen, story titles decided and we unlocked our door and.....

Nothing. And nobody. 'WHOOOOOOOOOO' went the tumbleweed....

'Ah well,' we thought, 'it's only the first day'....

Same the next, and the next. The site was empty. Everyone was away! And nobody had thought to tell us! HAHAHAHAAA. We didn't start till the week after schools went back, and the Travellers returned from...erm....travelling. So we sat. Chris dropped in with a couple of beers (which was nice) and we bunked off early – there was gin to be had and beans to cook....

Anyway, the next week, after another weekend of debauchery, too nameless and faceless to recount, I went back to Pikey School as we affectionately called it and there they were – all home. Or back. And all staring at the Unit and us in what can only be called a slightly puzzled look but with an undertone of menace and maybe even murder at the two gorgers that had suddenly appeared.

"Em. Hi! Hello! I'm, er...er...." Shit. Too gay. Lower your tone, Fotherington – Thomas. Man up a bit...

"Um. Hi. Erm, how do you do? So pleased to meet you. My name is......" Shit. Too posh.

"Um....Oright? Ah's it goin?..." Cockney! Brilliant! That'll warm their cockles....

"Who the fooking hell are YEW TEW?" Belfast!!! IRA probly.......

"What are youse doin on our saight? Nobody told us, so they did." (I think he must've meant 'so they DIDN'T', but I thought it best not to argue grammar at that point.)

"Well....we're teachers and erm...we're here to help your children erm...learn some....um....stuff...."

I trailed away into silence. This wasn't going too well.

"Is that raight? Wehl...... (Pease try to read this in a Northern Irish accent for a more authentic experience)....."*Can you teach may Mammy to fill in her dole form?"*

"Erm...yes, I suppose so....." (It wasn't on the curriculum, but in those days you could justify pretty much anything).

"And none of the wee ones can read. Can you teach them that? Eh? Can yew?"

"We'll try. Thank you, Mr. erm Traveller (for not slitting our throats and feeding us to your rather abominable looking dogs) *for being so erm...welcoming..."*

"Aye. Wehl."

And that was that. In.

The next few weeks WERE an education, but more for us really. Hardly anyone came for two days running, so all the lesson plans went to shit and anyway everything we had planned was completely irrelevant to their lives. It was no surprise the kids never went to school proper – it was meaningless to them other than as a socialising exercise but as they were all so self-contained, that seemed unnecessary too. I rather admired their community and the way in which they supported each other. It was just a bit difficult when, for instance, all we had for a day was a baby still in nappies, and 3 year old and an old lady who just sang all day and played with Lego. I am guessing this wasn't what Mark Carlisle had in mind as a beacon of Progressive Education or what Horace Cutler, head of the GLC at that time, was supposed to be spending his money on. However, if he ever wants to know how to cook a hedgehog so that all its spines come off in one go, I'm your man.....

The education authority soon caught on however - they had seriously miscalculated and the 'Traveller's Unit – Bringing Education Home' was a mahoosive white elephant. We jogged along for the term, teaching the intricacies of scamming the dole, claiming (we discovered) for kids that didn't exist or who were dead – they just wanted to know what the titles of the boxes on the form said and we dutifully read them out and in many cases actually filled them in, as nearly everyone was unable to write. Why would they need to, usually? They were on the road, working hard manually for a living – Reedin and Writin were of little value. Being loyal, however, was and we were, after that initial skirmish and they decided we were on their side – or at least, were being paid to help them, not punish or betray – and they were nothing but kind to us and helpful.

And so the term passed. A kind of Clark Kent existence – mild mannered professional by day, gin soaked trollop by night.....I didn't have a drink problem, though I realise it may sound as if I did – it was just that I COULD! No one was telling me what to do and it gave me courage, albeit of the Dutch variety, to be someone else. You see, I wasn't comfortable with Me, so I got pissed and pretended to be someone else! Genius! It was many many years before this situation changed.

There was, at that time, quite daringly, a darling little gay club just up the road. This was both good and bad. Good, because we had somewhere local to go and bad, because we went there every night and all weekend. Every weekend. Home from the Unit, beans on toast (sometimes with those little sausages in), large gin or two, change of clothes, into something gayer and off to Selina's went we! The kitchen window, which faced out to the road, bore witness to this as the empty Gordon's bottles filled the sill as testament to our recklessness.

The club was run by John, an East Ender, a Jew (his mother had been one, and after whom the club was named and with whom he had a very unhealthy relationship – she'd been dead years, and he had a little shrine with a hideous painting that he went and wept all over when things went wrong, which they did, often).

The club was in the cellar of an ordinary Victorian townhouse; just a brown door leading off the High Road. Opposite the nick! Blimey, you may say, but actually it was very handy – John kept them supplied with crates of lager and they kept an eye on us – turning out time was 11.pm of course but we always felt safe as we knew Lilly Law would be vadering from across the road.

It was just a room, windowless, airless and manky, with a little bar at one end and the bogs upstairs. But it was home. A refuge. A place of safety where we could let slip our masks, take off the armour we wore every day for protection. We could breathe, be camp, dance, snog, whatever. It was like our own front room but with more cock.

The Bar, Selina's, E11.

It was mixed, lesbians and fag hags and the occasional straight man or couple who lived near or who knew John. It was a family. We all knew each other and over the passage of time we had all shagged each other so there was no need for pretence. It was home. It was a place that, for me, at last, I didn't feel alone, the only gay in the village. There were LOADS of us! I was beginning to know WHHHOOOOO I was, WHHEERRRRE I was and that bruising, shameful and nightmarish night in Turnpike Lane began to fade – being queer didn't HAVE to be like that: frightening, desperate, unquestioning.

We looked forward to going, each night. We were welcome, and welcomed, Chris and I, and we were happy to be part of something. This was 1980, in the East End. Pretty revolutionary really but we never had any bovver. Maybe we were SO 'secret' there – it was like a Speakeasy at this point! – that nobody actually knew of its existence and all the queer bashers were up West, where, I heard tell, there were CLUBS and SAUNAS and FETISH BARS. That all seemed far away from our cosy little Cellar, our haven, our smoke filled hideaway.

What ALSO seemed far away was home. Home where my family was – I hadn't seen them or contacted them for ages - I was always too busy it seemed: a cock to suck, a lager to drink. It was, of course, deflection activity. THEY would be a reality I didn't want to face. For the first time I was doing what I wanted, no restrictions, no disapproval, no questions asked, no golden ear whizzes, which I most definitely would have got if my behaviour had been witnessed. But, they were 300 miles away, living in ignorance, and telling neighbours about their son who was *"teaching some gippoes up in London. What a marvellous thing 'es doing, educating people like that"*……the notion of racism, of xenophobia was

● ● ●

alive and well in the shires of my home land. Had they known how I was spending my 'non-contact time', then another kind of phobia would be in play. But, as I said, they were happy to think they had a son who was doing good in the world, being a Professional, being a beacon of virtue for the family (*'not like they other two, gettin' knocked up every five minutes, puttin' themselves about'*) – oh the irony! – and that's how I preferred to let it lie. I was finding an identity, of sorts. I had a decent job (which didn't last), I had money in my pocket (which didn't last) and I was young, free and single! (which also didn't last).

It was April 18th (my yellowed scrap of A4 wiv a pome on tells me so – and no, you're not reading it, you jeering crowd) and Chris, once again had something up in town and did I want to meet blah blah blah?

Remembering my last foray in to the world of drunken, puke laden 'romance', I was somewhat wary. *"Can't we go somewhere else this time? Somewhere a bit less...well, WHOREY?"* I asked Chris. *"Somewhere less......"*

"Less what? You got your end away, didn't you, last time?" I hadn't yet, out of shame, told him what had actually happened that night – he thought I'd pulled and should be bloody well grateful When I DID eventually tell him, he teased me mercilessly, doing pretty accurate Kate Bush impressions. The bastard.)

"Less what?"

I had an idea. *"Less common. Somewhere that does cocktails or something."*

"Oh fuck off you twat." (He was, by now, getting in to skinheadism and cocktails weren't exactly his scene. The 'cock' bit maybe.) *"This is London, mate, not fuckin Paris or poncey Hong Kong, or wherever they're supposed to serve poncey drinks. No. We're going to the Salisbury. You'll like it".*

"But....."

"No buts. We could go to the Dog and Trumpet on Great Marlborough Street cos that's near where I'm gonna be all day, but Salisbury after. I'm not going to the Pink Elephant 'cos that's for Poofs. If you get there first, mine's a lager."

DOG and TRUMPET? It sounded like a pub out of Dickens or something. But I looked it up in the A to Z and saw it was just off Oxford Street, easy to find from the Central Line tube. So, I got off work early (mostly because they'd all buggered off for the day, scrap hunting or something), got the tube into town and walked along Oxford Street, out and proud (ish) to the Dog and Trumpet.

• • •

It was nice. It was like a proper pub, all hanging baskets and the smell of fags and ale. A couple sitting outside, in business suits (Mmmmmmm yummy) talking and drinking, like erm...normal people. No sense of threat here...I got closer; one looked up and said, *"Alright, mate?"* and turned back to his friend. A woman turned up and sat with them, and they both kissed her Hello.

"You look a bit lost, mate. Want to join us?" one of the men said.

"I...erm...I'm waiting for....."

Then the other one turned round and he'd taken his work tie off, opened his top buttons and his magnificent hairy chest shone in the evening sunlight....

"Yes, I'd love to. Just while I'm waiting...."

Nigel Bray! You TROLLOP!! One glimpse of chest hair and you're anyone's!!

Actually, I wasn't, not that night, because a) the first bloke, introduced me then turned and kissed his mate/boyfriend/lover and b) Chris came hollering up the road, saying something like: *"They're WAAAY out of your league, you slapper! Sorry I'm a bit late. Ooo, I need a slash. Mine's a lager!"*

So we had a couple of pints in there and then suddenly the thought of entering Dante's Inferno seemed a much more attractive idea. So we walked along Carnaby Street (a shit strewn dump. I'm sorry, but it is!) and wiggled our way through the streets of Soho (with no inkling of what they would become.....) along Old Compton Street and out on to Charing Cross road, with its bars rapidly filling up with after - work boozers.

Threading through the alleys, we came out on to St. Martins Lane and there it was - the stained glass Deco doors, opening and closing, beery laughter spilling out on to the pavement.

Opposite there was another bar, seeming full of brazen homosexuals too! They were mostly what is now known as 'twinks', and all seemed to be squeaking and hooting at each other.

"Oooh! I never noticed this place before," yelled Chris. *"Let's go in here!"*

"I don't really think it's....." but he was gone, through the ultraviolet lit doors of 'Brief Encounter'.

I followed him in, squeezing between the jackets and the tied up vests of all the young queens thronging the entrance. And the bar. And the seating area. Blimey! So many homos in one place! (I was still such an innocent abroad...).

Chris was at the bar when I found him.

"Ah, there you are. Good. It's your round."

He, as per, went off 'for a slash', though I suspected he just went and hid round the corner till I got my wallet out. I looked around. It was really quite nice in here, the sort of place I could feel safe and normal. Admittedly, none of the men were my type - too young, too hairless and too, well, girly (Excuse me??)

By the time he came back, I'd got the drinks in and was looking around and all the twinkly twinks (who actually were not that much younger than me, once you got them in the daylight...) all gossiping and bitching. It was nice it was hummy and positive. We stood side by side, looking round and became gradually aware that we were being looked at, from behind hands, their courtesan fans and realised it was US that were being gossiped and bitched about - Chris in his drainpipe camouflage jeans, DMs and his green Harrington, me in my work Terylene trousers, stripy shirt, sensible shoes and carrying my briefcase.....this was the first inking I'd had that all poofs were not the same and even within our bruised and battered community, there was rancour and prejudice. I would discover, in my travels, that lesbians were not welcome in 'gay bars' (what?) that bears were not welcome at the twinky vest-tied discos, that Trans people weren't really welcome anywhere. To me, this was astonishing, and that night in the Brief Encounter, were the turds in the swimming pool.

"Chris. Come on, let's go. We're being stared at."

This was my first experience of 'homophobia', by my own people. How fucked up is that? *'I'm no different to you, you know! Same number of bollocks. Same age, ish. Same struggles, pain and victories. Love a willy, same as you....'*

This, this....injustice was running through my mind as we stood there, like two bacon sellers at a bar mitzvah.....why are you making these judgements? We're all gay, we all fought the same fight, faced the same demons, took the same brickbats.....why am I unwelcome here? If I put on some tight jeans and a lickle bitty vest thing, would you welcome me then? Same body, same person, different coating.....

• • •
13

I was, of course, being naive. This is how the gay scene was (and still is) - divided into little subgroups, and ne'er the twain shall meet. Bears and their cubs went to Bolts, the girls went to Gateways, the old guys and the rent boys went to the Elephant's graveyard on Bayswater road and the twinks came here. It was a scenario repeated all over London and any other town and city where there was a gay scene.

I, right now though, didn't know this. Didn't know that, actually though it goes against all the solidarity we fought for only a decade or so ago, it is actually OK. It enables you to be who you are, more clearly - I was beginning to figure out exactly who I wanted to shag (or, actually, be shagged by) and I knew it wasn't anyone here, in this neon lit, New Romantic playing hostelry. *'Don't you want me, baby? Oooh oo oo?'*......erm, no, actually, I don't, but there's no need to be quite so pissy about it. Each to their own, I say. But it was quite a sad shock to me at that moment to realise I was being ostracised by my own kind.

"I said, let's go," and I grabbed Chris's arm just as he was draining his pint. The lip of the glass slid off his mouth and a couple of gobfulls of lager cascaded down the back of someone's shiny jacket.

"Nooooooo! My coat. My best jacket. What have you done???"

Then he turned round and saw this 6'2" skinhead staring at him impassively and said,

"It's OK actually. I can get my Mum to wash it. Don't worry."

"Sorry, mate," said Chris. *"It was this fuckwit - he knocked my arm and......OI! Come here...!"*

But I'd fled. I couldn't stand the thought of the twinky bitchslapping Chris and Chris giving him a Glasgow Kiss or something. So, I left. I elbowed my shirty arms through the crowd, which began to part like the Red Sea to let this, this......'thing' not of us, through and I exited the twinky pinky palace and found myself, somewhat bewildered, out on the street.

"Oi, you twat. What's the matter? I hadn't finished me drink. Did you see his face when he turned round and saw me? Fuckin shit 'imself!"

I should point out here that Chris, far from being a bovver boy, a troublemaker, a hooligan, was a very well mannered, gentle man. He would never fight when words could do. He was too bright, too intelligent to get embroiled in any violence (though, years later, he did get smacked in the face by a bloke he'd got

● ● ●

off with in the club. They'd stumbled drunk up the stairs, out in to the street. They'd been all over each other like a rash and then Chris tried to get the bloke's cock out. Opposite the Nick. That didn't go down too well and he got a slap and a split lip. But, apart from that...) but he seemed to revel in this persona he'd created. Was this something that I would need to do, to be accepted 'on the scene'? I hadn't considered this – I thought you just held our hands up, said, "I'm gay!" and then just tried to get as much cock as you could. Apart from Mr. Carpetworld and the bloke at Turnpike Lane, I hadn't been hugely successful so far. Was that because I wasn't a 'BEAR'? Or a 'TWINK'? Or a 'LEATHER QUEEN'....? I, admittedly, always seemed to look like Clark Kent, all geeky with me briefcase, but inside I was...I was....

I had absolutely no idea.

I was 24, on a summer's evening in bustling London Town, outside a gay bar, in my work clothes, opposite a pub that had led to the worst experience of my life, with me best mate, and I suddenly realised – I was lost. In no man's land.

"What's the matter with you? Fuckin Friday night, work over, down the pub......fer fuck's sake. Cheer up!"

"I'm lost, Chris. I don't know who or what I'm supposed to be......"

"Oh, shut up, you twat. What you're supposed to be? You're supposed to be pissed, that's what! Come on!" and he dragged me out of my reverie, into the road, and over the Salisbury, with its gaping maw and promise of.....who knew?

I wanted to be loved, right? Basic human requirement. Like bread. Shelter. Beer. But those boyz in that bar weren't going to love me. And I didn't understand why. My rather naïve view was that if you were gay (not that I had much experience – wanking in the bushes at school camp hardly qualified, although I knew I liked it. A lot) and you wanted to have sex with other men, as long as you were willing and he was willing and you both had the right equipment, then what was the problem? Why did you have to be a 'type'? I'd seen the Village People, obviously but they were just a parody, a joke surely? There weren't really gay men like that? Why was one wearing a cowboy outfit? Why did that one have a leather cap and spiky wristbands? It was panto, surely? Chris was no fucking help, standing there in his 'uniform', his identity. Though I knew him better; had known him for years, knew this gentle and brilliant man who had crafted the witty and sparking music for *'The Common Room'*, all those years ago, who had eased me gently and wisely through my breakup with Slobbidbobbidy; though I knew Chris Hartley, this man, my friend, what the people passing by on this pavement outside Brief Encounter saw was someone they would probably rather avoid – a man of potential violence and trouble. So, HE had an identity, something he could shuck off and on as the need / party / trade required. But I, with my Terylene pants and stripy shirt (still clutching my briefcase. I don't know why I had it still, as it goes. The Travellers required few lesson plans and there was never any marking. Maybe it was MY badge, my way of saying "I have an identity! I'm a professional person") I didn't know where to fit. I knew who I fancied, the type, but I couldn't become one of those, in the way Chris could. He fancied skinheads, so he became one. I couldn't suddenly become hairy and butch. SO what to do? Were there places for 'my type'? Probably, but they would also be rich and young Turks, and I was neither of those things either.

"You OK? Really? Look, let's go in, and we'll find a seat (on a Friday evening? We'll be lucky!) *and I'll educate you, my dear little pooflet. Come on."*

So, once more, I stepped through those beautiful doors into what could be Heaven or could be Hell.

It was fuggy, it was comforting, it was pubby, it was thrumming with chatter and laughter and the clinking of glasses, all at different pitches depending on the amount of liquid they had in. the bar was packed, it was Friday, after workey-poos and people had been paid…..the night was yet young.

"This'll do. I need a slash. Mine's a lager," said Chris as he disappeared into the throng, which was actually very mixed.

There were no seats, but we found a space by one of the pillars; all carved in a spiral it was, with a little drinks shelf.

'THAT chat....'

When he came back and I had torn my eyes away from the chest hair of a man who was dressed in a silk blouse (I kid you not, dear readers) and a blonde wig, which set off his black beard in a very strange kind of way.

"Stop staring, fer fuck's sake. How old are you?"

I felt about 12. So naïve and unknowing. I thought it was all going to be so straightforward.

"Right. Now listen. On the gay scene, and I know, 'cos I've been on it for a few years and I've done and seen plenty, believe you me, there all sorts of groups, mostly based on sex and attraction. Like, I would never do one of them twinks over the road – not my type, see. And vice versa – specially that one you spilt my drink over! Hahaaaa. Anyway. Bears fancy bears. Twinks fancy twinks. Leathers queens, the same, Muscle Marys, ditto. Now, SOME twinks fancy bears and some chasers fancy cubs as they're sort of the same age. Some chasers fancy skinheads, but skinheads only fancy skinheads. Actually that not true, cos when I was in Norwich, I shagged a cub.

"What's a cub? What's a chaser? Why has everyone got different names? Why can't we all just like each other?"

I knew I sounded like Julie fucking Andrews, but it just didn't make any sense. I supposed I thought that after the agonies of my parting from my darling Bearsy, it would all fall in to place and I'd live happily ever after with a big hairy man in a world of lovely cuddly homosexualists. Apparently this was not the case.

...."*and in some lezzer bars* (Political correctness was never one of Chris' strong points), *the women dress up as blokes and their girlfriends are all lovely and girly. 'S true. They have suits and waistcoats and bloke's haircuts and even moustaches. Fuckin scary, some of 'em. PLUS...*".....he was in full swing now...."*blokes, even if they're poofs aren't allowed in their clubs and bars. Just get chucked out, you would or worse. Imagine bein' duffed up by a big lezzer! Avoid them places if you know what's good for you. Or maybe that's the problem. YOU'RE a lezzer!*" He cackled in to his glass, enjoying his joke immensely.

"Shut up, you knob. I need another drink. It YOUR round. YOURS."

"I know, I know, don't go on. I was just going!" And he went up to the bar. He soon came back with two fresh pints and said, *"You owe the barman £2.80. I couldn't find me wallet. I might've left it at school."*

Priceless. FUCKING PRICELESS!

So, I pay for the drinks (again) and we return to our conversation.....

"What did you mean about all those names for people? Cubs and otters and chasers and Muscle Martys. How do you know who fancies who? Are you allowed to fancy who you like? Like, what if you fancied a twink and you were a erm.....leather queer?

"QUEEN, you twat, not queer. And it's MARY not MARTY. Jesus. Well, of course you can fancy whoever you like. Nobody can help who they fancy can they? Trouble is, they got to fancy you back. You'd just have to go the right bar or club. Like Gateway, in your case. Pfffft! Hahahahaaaaaaa!" (Later, much later in this story, I do actually go and have a few drinks in The Gateway, with said 'lezzers', and very nice it was too.)

"Shut up, I'm being serious. What if I fancied someone and....."

"I could go over and tell him, like at school! Pahahaaa. Like last time we was in here. D'you remember? What happened with him, then? Was it good?"

Moving swiftly on....... *"Chris! Fuckin' LISTEN! What if I fancied someone, in here say, or in a club and I was getting all the right signals, how would I know what he was into?"* (Future proofing, against another Kate Bush moment)

"Well, you could just look at the hanky. That'd tell you."

"What? What hanky?"

Christ! Don't you know ANYTHING?? The hanky in the back pocket. Look, get me a pint, while I go to the bog and I'll tell you."

I went to the bar, again, wondering why, if we both teach, and earn similar salaries, I never have any money left and he seems to have plenty. I'm going to need to be Head of Education with the commensurate salary at this rate.....

"Right, are you sitting comfortably? Well, standing. Bollocks, I wish we could get a seat – me lallies are killing me. Oooooh look! There! By them two girls. We can squeeze in there!...............Hello girls! Room for two little ones?" and with that we left my education, and were sitting with two girls, who initially didn't seem too keen, but – remember we'd had about six pints by now, and we were just *HILARIOUS* – after a while kinda had fun. I never knew their names, but they were a blessed, if temporary relief from being exposed to the terrors of being a gay man. I felt about 12, I felt like Alice, lost in Wonderland where nothing was as I'd expected. They didn't stay long, not surprisingly....

Our New Best Friends, Salisbury Arms, W1.

"As I was saying, Mary," continued Chris after the girls had gone (escaped), *"you wear a coloured hanky in your back pocket, all different colours to say what you like and whether you give it or take it. It all started in America, in San Francisco. LOADS of poofs there, mate. All kinds."*

"Don't call me Mary, thank you. That's a girl's name". Honestly, talk about naïve. Gay men had been calling each other 'she' since time immemorial and gave each other girl's names. I have since found out that there is a gay

'language' called Polari which was used for secret communication between gay men, when being gay was illegal and punishable by imprisonment. It was common to call men 'she', and give them girl's names, particularly amongst celebrities Did you know that Elton John is known as 'Sharon, Freddie Mercury was known as 'Melina', Rod Stewart as 'Phyllis', Robert Plant as 'Elsie'...but I digress..

"Go on then, erm.....Doris. Hankie in pocket....."

"Oh yes. Those girls were nice weren't they? What were they called?"

"I don't know Chris. We were never introduced. You just went and sat on her lap."

"Well, YOU squeezed her tits."

"I DID NOT, you lying fucker! So…. HANKIES?

"Oh yes. Well, you wear a coloured hankie in your back pocket and each colour tells people what you like. You know, sex – wise. So, you see the hankie and if it's something you like, you know he does it. And Vicky vercky. Saves time. Like Morse code. Or something. Mine's a lager."

"TELL ME!"

"OK, OK. Don't get your knackers in a knot. Well, f'rinstnace, if you see a black one, you know he's into S+M. If you see a…."

"What's S+M?"

"Fuck me backwards. It's gonna be a long night….. SADO MASOCHISM, you knob head. You know, bondage, whips, cock and ball torture…."

Well, actually, I didn't know…..I was entering a parallel universe here, wandering paths that I didn't know were there.

"You mean, if he's got a black hankie, he wants to S+M you?"

Yes. YES. Jeeeze….

OK. What else?"

Yellow is for watersports."

"Cool! I'd like that! I suppose you'd have to go to Lea Valley, if you were in this area."

"No. Are you being a cunt on purpose? WATERSPORTS. Piss. He wees on you. Or the other way round. Depends which side the hankie is."

"WHAT? Wee? Like ......WEE?"

Deciding I was a lost cause, he ploughed on, hoping to get this over with so he could get another beer.

"If its red, that means fisting."

He must have seen my jaw drop and my mouth open to speak.

"Don't say another fucking word till I've finished. YOU wanted to know, so I'm telling you. Now pay attention so you don't make a cunt of yourself and end up in the dungeon in The Chain Locker with someone's fist up your arse because you haven't listened. I'm trying to save you from yourself.

So, red's for fisting – that where he puts his fist up your ass. Sometimes right up to the elbow.

If it's green he's a prozzy. A rent boy. Or you are of course, depending on the side.

Dark blue is just ordinary bumming. You know, anal.

Pink is for toys and dildo play. White is for just masturbation. Y'know, wankin' and that. Light blue is for gobblin'. Don't look so fuckin DIM! Oral. Gobblin'...."

I was finding it quite hard to take all this in.....yet I found the whole notion compelling - this was all going on, before my eyes, in the pubs and bars and on the streets and I HAD NO IDEA!! Nor did any of the public passing by...how ingenious! How deliciously secret!

"OK, last one. Brown. Now. What do you think brown might mean?"

He was delighting in my shock / fascination of this underground world and had obviously saved the best till last.

"Erm.....doing it with a black guy? Well, a brown guy......"

"No, that's only if you're a chocolate queen".

"What?"

"Chocolate Queen. You only go with BROWN blokes. Geddit? Usually 'cos they've got massive knobs. Allegedly. Same as Rice Queen."

* * *

"Uh?" I was losing my grip on reality.

"What do you think a rice queen is?"

"Someone who likes to have a Chinese takeaway with their boyfriend?" I ventured hopefully, but knowing I was doomed.

"Oh, fer fuck's sake. Who eats Chinese food with…..Jeeez. No. Only goes with Asians. Next. Bean Queen – only go with Hispanic blokes. You know – refried beans? Mexican grub?"

"Well, yes, but why………"

"Hummus Queen – only shags blokes from the Middle East. Spice Queen – only Pakis 'n that. Dairy Queen – whites only. Size Queen – big cock only."

"You're making this up. How do you know all this?"

"Ah, my little pooflet – so young, so innocent…Nah, it's all true. Can't be arsed with it meself. Don't care what colour or where they come from, if I like it, I'll shag it. Apart from you, obviously. Phahahahaaaaaaa", he cackled. He was clearly enjoying himself, both at being so knowledgeable and witnessing my astonishment.

"Now, where was I? Oh yes. Brown hanky. What do you think THAT might mean? Otherwise, known as scat."

"Oh I know that – it's like a kind of jazz singing. Cleo Laine does it. What's that got to do with sex?"

"HHHAHAAAHAHA" he cackled! "No! Brown is for scat. That's when you play with shit during sex. You know….butt fudge. You rub it on, or eat it or just have a wank while somebody has a shit. It's quite…"

But I'd gone. I was at the bar, out of earshot, my head reeling. Enough already. Some things I could visualise. Some sounded quite attractive. Some were a bit hard to know why you would want to do it, and each to their own. But eating turds was a step too far and I bottled it.

"Here. Here's a beer, so shut up now. Enough. Thanks for the lesson."

One more thing – make sure it's in the right pocket…..otherwise you might end up somewhere BOTH lying on your backs, both waiting for the other one. Thanks for the beer. Miss Helium Heels."

"Piss off."

It was now getting towards mid-evening and I'd been necking lager since teatime and I was feeling a bit swirly.

"I've had enough. Let's go home now."

"Fuck off! It's early. Get some crisps if you're hungry. Mine's cheese 'n onion."

I went to the bar (again) and managed to get some crisps. And as I stepped back from the bar, my arms held high above people's pints, my life changed. Blam, in that instant.

I trod on his foot as I stepped backwards.

"Oh, sorry, I didn't...."

"No problem...."

As I turned round, he said: *"Well, you're a cracker, and no mistake!"* (Really. He honestly said that!)

My heart stopped. The noise stopped. The room disappeared - no one else was in the room but the man who stood before me. Green eyes, with little flecks. Black hair. White teeth with a little nick out of one of the front ones. Blazing red tie, striped shirt. I took all this in in an instant. OH. My Bloody Fucking. Hell. He was THE most beautiful man I had ever seen, and he thought I was 'a cracker'.

"You alright?"

"Nnnnggggg."

"Can I join you?"

You can do whatever you want......even that brown thing. Skip or shat or whatever it's called. You could put your hand up my arse. You could....

"Um, yes, of course. Over here."

We crossed over to where Chris was, me with the crisps and this extraordinary man, and Chris with the bang needle as I'd been so long.

"Hello," said Mr. Gorgeous. *"Steve."*

"Hi," said Chris.

"Frluuuurrrrr nggggg," I said.

We sat, the three of us, not saying much, me not able to speak at all, and Chris resentful as he was no longer in charge of the situation. Steve schmoozed him, kept making little jokes, while RUBBING HIS FOOT AGAINST MY LEG!!! OH MY GOD!!! What to do? What would happen? I knew what I WANTED to happen but...

...years later – well an hour, I suppose - he said, *"Can I give you two a lift home? I've got my car and..."*

"Yeah. That'll be great," said Chris. I could see the signs, he'd had plenty to drink and was getting a bit belligerent, now his bestie had been stolen away.

We stood, me swaying a little by now, and followed Steve out of the pub and into the night. Somehow, on a Friday night, he'd found a parking space right across the road in New Row (My Stevie could do anything....) and so we got in his car, Chris, moaning, folded up in the back and me proprietorially in the passenger seat of the little Ford Fiesta. A Ghia. My man had a Ghia!

Soon we were speeding through the London streets, East along the A11 towards Stratford, blurred orange lights, blurred with beer, along the High Street and up Leytonstone High Road. I must tell you, dear reader, that he had his hand on my thigh all the time, in the darkness of the car and he kept scratching my right bollock with the fingernail of his left hand....I remember this, thirty four years on! It was one of the most thrilling, erotic, forbidden rides, full of fear, anticipation, joy, that I can ever remember (actually, not true – 2007 was a very good year. No! You'll have to wait.....)

We arrived home. There was no 'do you want to come in for coffee'. We all knew perfectly well there was no coffee on the menu. It was ME on the menu, and Chris wasn't invited to the table.

"I'm off to bed. Thanks for the lift. And don't make too much noise. I'm only in the next room and you're a noisy twat when you're getting shafted. Night." And he lurched off down the corridor to his room.

We stood in the hall. I was uncertain about how to proceed, but trembling with lust. We stood in the hall. His eyes were the most astonishing glittering magnetic....oh, stop! This all sounds like Mills and Boon, but I don't know how else to tell you. I couldn't move – they were tazering me to the spot.

Then he leant in, and with the gentlest of breaths, just ruffling the hairs on my neck, and said: *"Will you let me fuck you?"*

Just like that. No preamble, no build up, but….you know what? I didn't care! It was perfect, and a no-brainer – of course you bloody can!

So, we went to my shabby little room, closed the door, and…..

Now, what to do? Shall I tell you what happened? Shall I write a bonkbuster? Or shall I attempt to describe what this lovemaking was really like?

Votes counted. B.

We moved to the bed, which was by the window and the sodium vapour streetlights cast a honeyed orange glow around the room. We stood close, not yet touching, each just breathing the scent of the other. Slowly, gently as a breeze, he smoothed the skin of my face and neck as if to brush away all the disappointments of the past, the mistakes, the unfortunate times, to make it better, to make me believe that this COULD be real and right and perfect. A tremor shook me to my very core as I answered this call for absolution. This was not Turnpike Lane with its fear and stench of vomit and shame; this was not Pearcroft Road with its pain of loss, of defeat, of the destruction of hope. This was ……nowhere. This was a perfect cocoon of flesh and pale ochre light and the most beautiful man I had ever seen, just a breath away. I felt safe, I felt home, I felt whole and mended.

We kissed then, slow and bristly and full of urgent breaths. We sped up, in time with our rapid breath and swelling cocks, all time and thought eroded, and concentrated into this single moment.

I undid his blazing red tie. I unbuttoned his business shirt to reveal dark, dark hair, covering his chest, his belly and converging into a dark trail (Ahhhh!) which vanished into the waist of his trousers. His belt. His button. His zip. All slid open seamlessly to reveal his underwear, clean white and bulging with promise. The trail led under the waist of his pants and I traced it with my finger, underneath to where it was warm and urgent and, lifting the cloth away, I saw his cock. Large, slightly curved, fat and lost in a riot of dark hair.

I could barely breathe. This was the most perfect moment of my life. This stranger, almost naked, in my room, had come to tell me that everything would be OK, all the hurt and confusion would melt away and we would become one.

He undressed me too then, and we folded to the bed, entwined, urgent, naked, hard, hot and as one.

The sex was perfect. It was mine, it is private. And I shall stop here as I want that moment to remain as it was – secret, perfect and holy.

Mr. Lucky! Lucky Lucky *Lucky*!!

I include this because I think it shows how I felt that next morning. No it's not great poetry, it's a bit pretentious and a bit crap, but in the journey of this young homosexual, 24 years old and now completely in love, I think it tells you something, gentle readers, of the state of mind he was in.

Morning.

Shed light through the chink in the curtain.

Quietly as ghosts, my hands

Trace the swellings of your back.

Shadows. Hills tiny flecks of whiter skin where once you had chicken pox!

Oh glorious broad back!

Triangle made soft and round with curve

The light plays across it.

Further down. Further down.

Grey dawn light softly on your beautiful sleeping back.

Faint hairs like kisses spread.

Ass soft and paler

Beautifully shaped and dark with hair.

So as not to wake you

I trace the finely chiselled line of your spine,

Down and down, with butterfly nails and warm breaths.

Textures changing now for used

To softness of hair and ass

From muscled and sun – browned

To pale swelling curves.

I wish I could draw you

Or keep you beautifully there

To look at 'til I'm old.

April 18, 1980.

OK, a bit naff, but that's how it was. I was full of his semen and full of wonder at the presence of this man in my bed. New. Unique to me.

Eventually he woke, morning wood, and a smile. I wanked him off (it would have been rude not to) and he got up to go to shower to head back. Back to….back to? Where? Where was he going, actually? Its Saturday morning….

"Oh I need to get back home for the weekend. Can we meet Monday?"

Monday? MONDAY?? That was aeons away! MONDAY????

"Well, OK then but….where's 'home'?...."

He put his finger on my lips and held me with those eyes……

"Sshhhh….Monday. Outside Centrepoint. I finish at five. "

A brief kiss, a flash of red tie and he was gone, leaving me standing on the edge of a massive void. What was I going to do until MONDAY??

Chris emerged from his room.

"Smarmy boy gone then? Fuck and go, was it?"

"No, ACTUALLY. We're meeting again on Monday, in the City. ACTUALLY. "

"He's a bad 'un. He won't turn up."

Yes he will. Why are you being so shitty? 'Cos I got a boyfriend, and you haven't?
(God I can't believe I said that. I sound like I was 12!)

"He's not your boyfriend, you prat. He wanted a bed for the night. And a shag. And he got both. Just smile and say thank you."

"He'll BE there. And so will I."

"Where's he gone now then?"

"He's...erm....I don't know actually. Home. He said he had to go home."

"Huh. Probly got another lover at home. "

"Fuck you. I love him, so stop....."

What I said next was drowned out by the gales of laughter coming from Chris.

"Love him? You've only known him 10 minutes!"

"Yes, but we made love. I gave him my soul......."

"Oh fuck off. You're a dopey cunt and it'll be ME who'll have to be here to pick up the shit. Again."

And he slammed the door back in to his room.

"OOOOOOh , bitchy......."

But he didn't reappear.

The weekend dragged by. We went up the club. We got pissed (no change there then) and everyone was saying *'what's the matter with you? What are YOU grinning about'* and I'd say: *"Oh nothing. Well, actually, I have a boyfriend. He's gorgeous and I love him and I've only known him a little while, but we're in love and we're meeting on Monday at Centrepoint because he works in the city and he's got green eyes and lovely hairy belly and he thinks I'm a cracker and...."*

Eyes glazing over......and I didn't even notice HA HA!!

We watched telly.

I watched the clock. I tried to do some lesson plans but they were shit. I decided to do the ones I did last week as nobody was going to turn up anyway. Addin' up. That'll do.

We watched the telly.

We went up the club. We got pissed. I didn't get off with any one as I was now, in my eyes, practically married and only wanted my Steve. My Stevie.

Monday came. I went to the unit. I did...some stuff. I watched the clock. 2 0 clock. 5 past 2. 3.0 clock. 5 past, 10 past. 3.15.

"Yeah, bye! Bye everyone! Byeeee!"

SPEED!

Speed up that hellish road at dawn,

Crash, Icarus, into my weekday waiting arms!

I wait! I want.....

I was out of that classroom before they'd even put their books away. Along Crownfield, up the high road, on the tube, off the tube, at Centrepoint . In a blur.

So. Hartley was wrong. (Thank God)

Here you are,

Brown, and full of careful touches

(more careful than when you left)

(May 13, 1980, scribbled on an envelope, to preserve this moment. Sad, I know!)

"Hi."

"Hi."

Two small words, one contract.

Wee'd a bit.

"Salisbury?"

"OK."

Off we went again, threading through those now familiar streets and alley, through those now familiar doors.

"Pint?"

"Um, yes please."

"I'll bring it over."

"OK."

Not the most scintillation of conversations but I was pretty much struck dumb. Just his presence, his walk, his solid legs as they splayed as he sat, his scent, his eyes. Oh god! His eyes.

I will move on from this episode soon, I promise. When you started this, I am assuming you weren't expecting a Barbara Cartland scenario. You wanted more shaggin', more swearin'......But this is what it was....pure Mills and Boon.....'Handsome man gets his conquest to swoon a lot'. That was what happened. I felt entirely helpless in his presence. I would have walked hot coals, eaten a new born infant if he had asked. I was utterly, utterly enraptured. I felt sick and dizzy and hot and fearful.

Anyway – I shall move this on towards its conclusion – we had a couple of pints and he said,

"Hungry? I haven't eaten yet."

"Erm Yes."

"Come on then."

We left the pub, into his car, hand resting on my thigh as he drove one handed. So proprietorial! We pulled in to the Angus Steak House on Stratford High Road, where he treated me to dinner, bought wine and began to talk....

I'd never been treated like this. Like a lady. As it were. Considered, complimented, fussed over. Better than beans, I can tell you.

Anyway, in his gentle West Country burr, he began to talk. He was from Dorset, he played the organ (no laughing at the back!), he was 'a bit older than me', he had a house down West, he worked for an electronics video thingy in London.....I was interested – it was good to know about the man I was going to spend the rest of my life with, after all. He liked fine wines, dining out – I suspect the Angus Steak House was NOT where he would have chosen but it was on the way home – and he thought I was a cracker. Actually he didn't say that, but he must've, because he was, buying me dinner and taking me home.

We went back to the flat. Chris was in the lounge.

"Sorry I missed tea! Steve took me to The Steak House. It was very nice actually!" I trilled.

"Great."

"Night then!"

We went straight to bed and fucked our brains out. TMI? Sorry, but there it is. None of the gentle caressing of the first time this was full on, animal fucking. Enough detail right there. And I loved it. And I loved him.

And this continued, every night until Thursday. Friday morning he said,

"See you Monday, I have to go home for the weekend."

"Can't I come? I'm Cornish, it would be nice to go down West."

"No, sorry. See you Monday, same time, same place?"

"Okay. I lov……."

Slam. Door shut. My love gone.

"You're a dopey cunt," said Chris.

"Charming. Bit jaloose, are we?"

"Of him? Nope. Just worried for you. You don't even know him."

"I know he loves me." I was sounding like a child……

"Has he said so?"

"Well. No. but, he acts like he does."

"Oh for fuck's sake. He buys you a burger, shags you and gets a free bed."

"It was STEAK, actually. I know he loves me. I can see it in his eyes."

"You can't see further than the end of his dick. He's USING you."

"Go fuck yourself."

Hurt that my best friend wasn't happy for me, I slammed off into my room, like a hissy queen. How DARE he say these things about my Steve?

Chris, darling Chris. Wise Man. Why didn't I listen?

• • •

This went on for a couple of weeks: Centrepoint, pub, meal, fuck.

"Tomorrow. Same time, same place"...

Nothing changed though, moved forward. On Friday mornings, we would agree to meet on Monday as 'he had to go home for the weekend'.

Now, Chris, and probably all of you, could see what was happening here, but he was right, I WAS a dopey cunt, too blinded by semen and body hair, and someone with a few quid to chuck around to even SUPSECT what this all might mean.

The following Monday, I went up West a bit early, and walked down Charing Cross Road from the direction that he always seemed to appear from, and there, a few shops in, was......oh I don't know! This was 35 years ago!....a shop selling video equipment. So I went in.

"Hello. Does Steve..erm...." Fuck! I didn't even know his surname! And it was going to become mine!! I'd better find out!!....*erm...Steve work here?"*

"Yes," said the miserable tart on the desk. *"He's just coming down."*

And did. There he was, red tie blazing, striding down the stairs like a Colossus! Legs, strong and dependable.

Oh. Hello. Erm...what are you doing here?" Slightly panicky, I thought...

"I thought I'd come and surprise you!"

"Is this him?" said Tracey (let's call her that). *"Not worth losing Ian over, I don't think."*

"Shut the fuck up!" said Steve, and dragged me out of the shop and along the road.

Ian?

    Ian?

       IAN??

          IAN???

             IAN????

• • •

"Who. Is. Ian?" I asked, although I already knew.

"Oh, he's my friend. Down West."

"Your FRIEND. Define FRIEND……"

"Well. Um, he's……he's….."

"YOU FUCKING FUCKING FUCKING BASTARD CUNT SHIT," I screamed, in the middle of Charing Cross Road.

"He's your fucking boyfriend, isn't he? THAT'S why you go home every weekend. You fuck me Monday to Thursday, and fuck him at the weekends. Very convenient. VERY FUCKING CONVENIENT. YOU FUCKING FUCKING BASTARD!!!"

"Can you be quiet? Everyone's looking!"

"NO I FUCKING WELL CAN'T. I LOVE YOU. YOU CUNT, I LOVE YOU. HOW COULD YOU? HOW FUCKING COULD YOU?" Hurt beyond words, sobbing, red, and standing, beaten and bleeding in front of a bookshop that sold novels about this sort of thing.

"No, were not together anymore. I mean, I don't love him or anything. We just live together now. Nothing's going on. Now, please stop yelling and let's go home."

*"FUCK OFF FUCK OFF FUCK OFF FUCKK OFF,!!!!!"*I bellowed and turned and ran back to the tube and went home.

Sobbing all the way from the tube to home – a good mile or so, ignoring the stares – I arrived back at the flat, opened the door and there was Chris. He took one look, opened his arms and in to them I fell.

"Ah, so soon. So soon. Be still, and I will comfort you".

Mr Lucky had left the building.

How Chris coped with me during the next few days will always remain a mystery, and one for which I remain eternally grateful. The comforting arms, the cajoling, the bollockings – all served to stitch the gaping wounds left by Steve, my Stevie. *HOW* hadn't I seen what was happening? Chris had, *YOU* had….I was so blinded, and blindsided, by my feelings for him, the amazing sex, the beauty of his body and the astonishing power of his eyes that I couldn't see, or even imagine, that there would have been anyone else. He loved *ME*. He must've because he took me out, he made love to me properly with gentle touches and whispering breaths. There couldn't be anyone else. "Would the winner of the 1980 Miss Naivety Award please step forward".....

I thought back to Chris saying: *"He buys you a burger, shags you and gets a free bed."* and I squirm with embarrassment both from knowing he was so so right and also because of the way I responded to his somewhat clumsy attempts to save me. I know, looking back, that my willingness to be entirely subsumed by Steve's attentive kisses and promises (though he didn't actually MAKE any) was an attempt to validate what I'd done to Julie, to prove to myself that all the blood and pain was worth it. I COULD be gay and happy – it wasn't the oxymoron it seemed before. I was bad to him, and assumed he was just pissed off 'cos I had a bloke and he didn't, whereas really he was projecting forward to an event he knew would come and to preparing himself for a massive amount of 'there there-ing', which, as he knew it would, came quite soon and quite suddenly.

Before I round off this 'series of unfortunate events', there is a little postscript.....

A few days later, Steve appeared at the door. There was a knock, and I went, expecting HIM to be the last person I'd see, but, no, there he was, and all the hating and swearing and the collection of pins for my imaginary voodoo doll fell away.

"Oh. Um....Come in."

"Thanks."

"Why are you here?"

"To explain."

"Nothing TO explain. You have someone else. That's it."

"No, that's NOT it. Can I come in?"

"If Chris finds you here....."

He stepped through the door and back into my bedroom and into my heart.

We spent some time talking...all the usual old bollocks about how he'd never meant to hurt me (he did), about how he was going to tell me (he didn't) , about how he didn't really love him, he loved me (he didn't), and how he was really really sorry...(he was. I think). I wasn't sure what to say. He kept looking at me, pinning me down, and crying. Yep. Crying. If you'd known him, you'd know what an unlikely event that was, but he was genuinely upset. Why? Who knows? Because I was so hurt? Because he'd lost his weekday shags? Because he would now have to pay for B+B, or find another 'cracker' in a pub? Or, as I really wanted to believe, because he did have real feelings for me, if not Love, and he was sorry it had all ended so badly, right there in the street.

"So, what do you want to explain, Steve?" My heart was thumping, gasping with the thought he might say he'd left HIM, and he wanted to be with me…

"Erm…..I should have told you. It started off as just sex, cos I really fancied you. Still do, actually. But then I started to get feelings I couldn't afford. I have a house, a lover and another life in another place and I can't have both. I tried. For a bit. But you were becoming more and more important and I had to choose. It wasn't meant to come out like it did. That silly bitch on reception…..but….well, it did. Ugly. And you can certainly swear when you want to eh?"…hand crept on to my knee…..it was quite sexy actually. *"Look, I'm shit at this, but I just thought I owed it to you to say goodbye, properly, not just disappear. So, here I am. Can I stay? Just once more. Last time…?"*

Then, inevitably, like there nothing else ever, we went to bed. The last look at this body I adored; it was SO painful I could barely move but he was already undressed, and hard before me. I had no choice. Literally, I could not chose not to. He was my crack, my heroin, my opiate of choice.

"Will you fuck me?" he said.

Astonished, I stared at him. It had always, always been the other way round. I wasn't even sure I could.

"Please. Don't ask why, because I don't know, but fuck me. Please!"

So I did, dear reader. My first deflowering. My hankie had moved to the other side! It was a very strange experience – amazing, beautiful, but strange – and I know that I hurt him, but we continued, I came, he came and we collapsed, exhausted to the rumpled sheets.

"I think it's best if you don't mention this to anyone, OK?" And I haven't. Not till this very day, when it doesn't really seem to matter much anymore. It was glorious and blissful and unexpected. I gave him my soul and my seed as parting gifts.

• • •

In the morning, he dressed, stood by the bed, and said: *"In a different time, a different place, you would have been mine. I could have adored you. Be lucky next time."*

And bang! Slamming of the door, the flash of red tie and he was gone. For ever. Well, for the next ten years, but that's a different story. Chris came out of his room – he must have come home sometime during the night.

"Who was that?"

"Oh. Steve."

"STEVE???"

"Oh, don't worry about him," I said. *"He's fucked."*

And he was.

CHAPTER TWO.

THE ONLY WAY IS ILFORD.

<u>In which our hero meets his love, his nemesis and gets adopted.</u>

'Upside Down'.

by Diana Ross. No.3. August, 1980.

Absolutely head over heels....upside down and every which way, for sure.

~ ~ ~

Selina's, with its decks blaring *'Caribbean Queen', 'Move Closer'* and *'RELAX!'* (which is the best single EVER made, incidentally) became my source of comfort. The massive hole that Steve had left, even after such a brief encounter, was weeping and not healing too well, in spite of Chris' administrations of gin and admonstrations of *"Stop fuckin mopin' about. I told you he was a twat, and so were you for not listening. Let's go up the club. Mine's a lager"* (– I know you were trying to be helpful, but...really. You weren't.). So beer and sex were the order of the day – or rather, evening. School had to be gone to, kids, grans and all between still had to be tended to, reports prepared for the LEA....when I felt least like it. My heart was broken – it was, so don't laugh. It was a searing, unceasing ache which I sought to calm with lager and cock, pints and penises. It worked for the times I had both in me, but the morning came, the sun rose again and the pain returned.

The only even remotely amusing interlude from this bleak time was what I will call *'The Night of the False Alarm but a Good Chance to Cop Off'*. We'd been up to the club; it was a busy night, the music too loud, the trade all dressed up, the bar too pushy but I wasn't bothered. I was sitting morosely by the PacMan table, downing pint after pint, as if by filling myself up with liquid, it would flush my sorrow away. I would piss him down the toilet. Which is where my life was...... Who could I shag to ease the pain tonight? I looked blearily round the smoky room. Unfortunately I'd had most of 'em and the ones I hadn't weren't particularly interested in a mopey queen who was always on the verge of tears. Or suicide. Or something.

"You're a bundle of laughs. Why didn't you stay home? You're putting me off me beer. Fuckin' cheer up. Get a shag. Or shut the fuck up."

"Chris", I tried to say, through lips and a mouth that wasn't functioning too well. *"I'm upset. What he did n everyfing. He a fuckin shut. And a manker."*

"WANKER, not MANKER. You Wanker. Hahhhaaaa.Bit pissed are we? I was going to get a round in, but I think I'll get you home. Boring cunt. Come on, get UP!"

And he pulled me to my feet. The PacMan table was fortunately at the bottom of the back stairs and so I was able to get up and out to the pavement before I threw up several gallons of lager, over my trousers, my shoes and the pavement.

"Nice. Come on. Home." And he escorted / marched me the few hundred yards back to the flat.

When we got back, he began to run a bath. *"You stink of puke. Get in the bath. I'm going to have a fag. I don't suppose we've got any gin left?"* This was a rhetorical question, obviously. I went into the bathroom, had the brilliant idea of getting in fully dressed – I reasoned that, as my trousers had sick all down them as well, I might as well wash them now. So in I got.

I must have fallen asleep, or passed out, but the next thing I heard is a BANG BANG BANG on the door and Chris yelling, *"Just coming!"* I got out of the bath, and in a towel wrapped round me, even though I was fully dressed, and feeling really REALLY shit, went out in to the passage. There was Chris, in his really really short dressing gown (what time was it? I must've been in there for hours? Presumably he'd been checking I hadn't drowned?...) opening the front door.....the windows on the street side were lit up with flashes – blue, white, blue, white – and I looked out of the kitchen window and THERE WERE TWO FUCKING GREAT FIRE ENGINES PARKED OUTSIDE!!! Meanwhile, about 15 firemen, in full breathing gear were piling in to our tiny hallway, pushing Chris up against the wall and causing me to retreat into the bathroom. The lounge door was opposite the bathroom door so I could see. They were searching round, flashing torches and yelling at each other: ALL CLEAR! BEDROOM ALL CLEAR! KITCHEN ALL CLEAR! One looked at me, in my soaking clothes and towel, raised his eyes to Heaven, and turned back. BATHROOM ALL CLEAR!

Wingfield Rd. My room, bottom left.

They began to leave the flat. And I kid you not, Chris was standing in the hall, with a huge erection poking out of his dressing gown (which barely covered his ass cheeks anyway) talking to one of them, who later, *sans* uniform came back, a couple of hours later (when he'd finished his shift, one would hope), and fucked him. Never one to miss a chance, our Chris. Anyway. The final fireman to leave came out of the lounge and doing his best to ignore Chris's stiffy and, holding up the wicker wastepaper basket in one hand and a fag end in the other, said, *"It would be good if you could ensure you've put your cigarettes out before you throw them away. Thank you, and good evening erm...gentlemen."*

"Oooo, sorry Sir. Silly me. I'll be careful next time. 'Night."

And they left. Chris collapsed laughing. *"That was fuckin funny weren't it?"*

"Well, yes. I suppose so. Although we could have been burnt alive."

"You were alright. You were underwater....." and he cackled and roared and lit another fag.

I wobbled off to bed, but I dimly remember hearing the doorbell again and Pugh, Pugh, Barney McGrew, Cuthbert, Dibble or Grub coming back to put Chris's fire out with what was undoubtedly an enormous hose.

This misery went on for months (WAY too long, Chris said); spring passed, Easter came, term ended, caravans disappeared, never to be seen again......when we reconvened for the Summer term, NO ONE came back. The whole camp was down in Kent picking hops, and there they stayed....nobody told us, but there was no one to teach and no date as to when they might be back. So, my brief sojourn into educational right – on – ness abruptly ended with a transfer down to E13...Prince Albert Dock, the 3rd circle of Hell, from which I promptly resigned – it was one flying jam jar too far, but...more of that later.

New job. Being back on London transport didn't serve to enhance my mood. Eternally gloomy and sad, I sought refuge in *'Sooper Trooperper'* and hoped its lights weren't gonna find me, by not going to *'Funkytown'*, by not *'Standing So Close to'* the Police and by not being *'A Woman In Love'* any more.....it was all shit, tbh. I was SOOO fucking miserable and everyone seemed to be against me – they knew I'd been a twat and gave me little sympathy and it all just seemed so unfair. I'd given up a whole life to live this one and now I'd been shat on, from a great height. I wanted to 'end the heart-ache, and the *'thousand natural shocks that flesh is heir to'.* I just wanted it to stop HURTING. Boo hoo.

So, my master plan seemed to be to drink lager. And lots of it. That doused the pain temporarily, but as we all know, it's still there in the morning, coupled with a banging head and occasionally some love bites of an unknown origin. I realise this may all sound a bit dramatic – as dear Chris said: *'You'd only known him five minutes',* but that was NOT the point. The love I'd had for him was fierce, unquenched and, in addition it had reopened the careful stitching of my separation from Julie, which was still fairly recent, although gin and sex had kind of erased some of that. Given my miserable experiences thus far – viz: a wank in a carpet store, a night with Kate Bush on smack and my heart broken by the most beautiful man I'd ever seen, and who I'd even fucked, all in the space of a few months....maybe this was God's way of telling me NOT to be a homo. Maybe it just wasn't for me. Maybe I could go back to Julie, back to solidity, to familiarity – my family will be happier, my Dad wouldn't have apoplectic fits of homophobic fury when he found out – he need never know!, Julie would welcome me with open arms and all this pain would cease. It was reducing me, lessening my ability to function at work and reducing my perception of what would be wise when I had my beer goggles on. Maybe THAT'S what I should do. Go back. Stop whoring. Stop drinking and it will stop hurting.

I was having these internal dialogues, during the times I was sober enough to think coherently; I began to go to the club a little less often, drink less, eat better – in preparation to begin my new old life. I began to feel better, and began to make plans (I hadn't told Julie about this yet, but she was BOUND to want to. Wasn't she?) And then, on August 8th, 1980, I went to Selina's, bright eyed, bushy tailed, full of focus and light of heart.

And that was the night I met Rod.

'Friday night, just got paid. I'm runnin wit my mans, we got plans of gettin laid' as Johnny Kemp once said, only I wasn't runnin wit my man cos I didn't have one. I'd had Steve, and he'd fucked off and I'd had pretty much everyone currently in the club. (Don't judge! So had everyone else – it was a family thing...) SO it was likely to be a usual Friday: beer, couple of quid in the fruity, some dancing, and not *'Usin' It Up' or 'Wearin' It Out'*, which was No1 that week which usually meant Carlos would play the bastard thing every other record, as he seemed to think he was the world's number one record promoter. Some more beer, some chat with the regulars, seeing who'd had who since last Friday, some beer, moaning about the music, moaning about the weather (which was wonderful early August sunshine, but that wasn't the point), moaning about those people over there for being so noisy and for having such a good time. So far, so normal.

That night however, there was a group of people I'd not seen before – brash, self-confident, loud but somehow a welcome addition to the general melee of tired old queens and bright young things having a few stiffeners (ooh missus) before heading up West for a night of discoing and shagging, and more besides – I'd had 'the Talk', remember......

I was fascinated by these people, and by one in particular. Was he handsome? God, no. Balding, big nose, strange teeth.....a kind of gay Fagin. But he had this kind of....stuff around him, this aura, which made him the centre of the little universe he was in. He looked across the room, and his smile, so wonky and odd, seemed to carry with it all the love of the world. The woman, who seemed to be his sister, clearly adored him as did the little fat chap with them. The room kind of grew quiet, the music seemed to dim and just hover in the background – while I watched them. And watched them.

My Nemesis, my drug.

"Who are they? Over there, by the stairs?" I asked.

"Dunno. Never seen them before," said Ian.

"Dunno, but they were here last week," said Pete.

"They were? I never saw them."

"That's because we went up West, you knob," said Chris in his charming fashion.

Yes, indeed we did. This is what happened. We'd gone to The Pigeons, on Romford Road, a great cavernous place that looked to be an old ballroom. It was manky and smelled of wee and fags. (Cigarettes, I mean.). It had a licence till 1. a.m., pretty radical for the time at least, for somewhere not Up West. We'd gone after the club, which probably was a mistake because a) we were already pissed and b) we had hardly any money left. Anyway, we paid our £1 entrance fee (I kid you not) – you had to pay to get in because they served 'food' – I say that loosely - as a part of their licencing agreement, and climbed the sticky stairs to the bar room bit.

"You'll be having lager then Chris, will you?"

"I thought it was MY round, but yeah, OK then. Cheers!"

The Pigeons.

We stood around a bit, listened to some awful stuff apparently called 'Hi NRG', which seemed to be the only option lately and I wondered what we were doing here. Chris, who'd done his usual disappearing act, suddenly came back and said:

"Come over here. Meet these two blokes I've met."

Oh God......fearing the worst, I followed him and there were, indeed, two 'blokes' smiling at us. I have no recollection of their names but Tarquin and Oliver will suffice.

"This place is a fucking dump, yah? Would you like to come up town with us?"

Why they would have asked US, I have no idea, but before I could even open my mouth, Chris said, *"Fuck yeah! Come on!"* and before I knew it, we were outside the pub, standing next to an open topped yellow Porsche. *"Come on chaps, in you pop!"* said Tarquin. Or Oliver.

"Yeah, come on you twat! Don't just stand there..." and the next thing I knew, we were hurtling down Stratford High Street towards God knows where. After a very scary drive through the freezing night air, everyone screaming,

> *We're gonna use it up - wear it out*
> *Ain't nothin' left in this whole world I care about*
> *I said one two three shake your body down'*

 to the pounding car stereo, and then suddenly we screeched to a halt in Oxford Street,

"Come on chaps, Out you pop!" said Oliver. Or Tarquin. *"We're here."*

'Here', was 'SPATS', a night club which opened until 04.00 and it was only half past twelve! Hurrah! Three and a half hours in a cellar with no money. Brilliant Chris. Am I allowed to use the word CUNT here? You know I don't normally swear, but....Tarquin and Oliver had disappeared and so there we were, no drink, no money and no way of getting home. An excellent end to a night out. Nice one, *HARTLEY*.

In the end, the plan we came up with was as disgusting as it was inevitable: we each started chatting up a bloke, a drunk one, who was in a group of drunk ones and we persuaded them to let us go to the bar and get a round of drinks with the money they gave us. But, instead of going to the bar, we legged it up the stairs and out in to the night, bought a kebab and got the night bus home. I've done some really horrible things, eh? I'm not a bad man.....it's just that I find myself in extremis sometimes, mostly due to my friend....

Anyway, back to the Club, on this Friday night...

"Oh. Right. Well, who are they?"

"I don't fuckin KNOW! Shall I go ask them?"

"No. No, its fine."

"OK then. I'll have a lager, I need a wazz," and he went over the stairs, that led up to the bogs. As he passed the group, he leant over to them, and said something and went up to the toilet.

When he came back, he said, *"The ugly one's Rodney, his sister's called Kath and the fat ones is Milly or Missy, or something. OK?"*

"Erm, yes. Thanks. I didn't really want you to...." but he'd gone to play Pac Man to see if he could beat my high score (he never did).

Friday night wore on, *Creeping in this petty pace, to the last syllable of recorded time*; drinks were drunk (as were people), faces were snogged, crotches were fondled, and lurching dances were attempted, and still, STILL he sat there, with his *coterie*, drinking his lager, smoking his St. Moritz (oh God. Cool. As.), laughing and just occasionally looking over the bench seat that ran along the wall, where I was sitting – having none of the aforementioned options. Apart from the beer.

● ● ●

And then. Then. *'Dap dap…..dabbadabbadabbadabba doo doo. When the dark is callin…..'*

"I fuckin LOVE this song!" yelled Rodney and suddenly came through the throng, towards me and dragged me out on to the tiny, jostling dance floor.

Carlos had turned it up to 11 and I found myself suddenly in the arms of this strange man, who had hips like a snake and a generous bulge in his white jeans. *"George Benson 'Gimme the Night',* he yelled. *"My favourite! Well, apart from Alma Cogan. Oh, and Della Reese."*

> *'Cause there's music in the air,*
>
> *And lots of lovin' everywhere*
>
> *So gimme the night! Boop boop…….'*

he bellowed, in my ear. And now, 34 years later I can still hear him, still smell his 'Habit Rouge', and feel his heart beating against mine. 'Dababababababaa Boop Boop!' sends me back to that dive, that smoky room and the night I met the man I would love with more passion than I knew I had in my soul.

The music ended. We stood still. I was wearing ridiculous fawn elephant cords and a green open necked t-shirt, and looked like a twat who'd put on whatever'd been lying about, which I had. He looked impossibly cool – white jeans, proper leather jacket. None of yer plastic schmutter.

"Well," he said. *"Do you fuck, or not?"*

Clearly I did, because when I woke the next morning, in the usual 'where the bleddy hell am I, bad hair' sort of way, which was quite a common occurrence, sad to report, I looked over and there he was, still asleep, chest rising, falling with his breath. I was captivated by this man – in the cold, club -lightless light of day, he seemed to me to be a child, and boy / man, who needed to be healed from some terrible hurt, though I didn't know what. He had a beautiful thick mat of chest hair – not thick and curly, but striated, like proper hair. It was so magnificent, so masculine, and it converged into a deep dark trail down his belly (Ah! Joy!) and into a riot of dark hair surrounding a generous cock. Not Jewish, then. Captivated. Marvelling. Waiting. Not knowing what to do. I didn't even know where I was, but it didn't matter. I wasn't going to nick cash from his wallet; I was going to wait to see who he was, this man who took me to his bed. I have no recollection of the sex we had – too drunk, too tired – but residues proved that we did.

"Morning," he said, opening his eyes and catching me staring.

"Oh, Morning, " I said, startled, caught in the act. *"OK?"*

"Yes. You?"

"Yes, I'm. Erm...fine. Thanks."

"Sleep well?"

"Erm, yes. Thanks. You?"

"Yes, very well".

"Looks like another hot one...."

"Yes. Seems so. It's only early too..."

This was beginning to feel a bit embarrassing - should I just say, *'I'll ring you'*, and leave?

"Great fuck, wasn't it?"

"I.....um.......god yes," I stumbled. *"Beautiful"* and then, to my horror, blushed like a girl.

"I hope I didn't hurt you? I was a bit erm...insistent. Just that I really fancied you."

'Fancied'. Past tense. Here we go then. I'll get me coat.

"No. No, it was....great. Really." Actually, I was feeling a bit.....used in the bottom department, but I didn't mind. Didn't mind that it was HIM that had caused it.

Long pause.

"How old are you, Nige?" Nige? NIGE? How did he know my name....that fucking Chris I bet. If I find out he'd said *'My friend over there fancies you'*, making me sound like a 12 year old..... And anyway, I didn't. Then.

"I'm 24."

"WHAT? Oh FUCK FUCK FUCK."

"Why, how old are you?"

"36. This'll never work."

"Why? Why not?"

"Well. Well, because…." But he didn't finish because I kissed him, and he kissed me back as if his heart would break. A pause. A long stare and then:

"KAFF! KAFF! I must be meshugena, KAFF!!! Can Nige stay for breakfast?" Then he said, *"Do you want to move in?"*

Boom. Just like that.

"OK. Yes. Why not?"

And so began four years of joy, pain, heartache and wondrous love.

Rod and me, Selina's. 1980

Theirs was a big family. Bit of Jewish, plenty of Cockney. Dad had died not long before I met Rod, a part of his sadness, I think but there were still Mum – Big Kit, a darling matriarch if ever there was one, 4 sisters, another brother and Rod, not to mention numerous uncles and aunts and cousins, all dotted around the East End and always in and out of the house, in Ilford. All Jewish, all East End born and bred and bleedin' diamonds, all of 'em. They took me in, without missing a beat, because Rod asked them to, because I was Rod's new partner and so it was OK with them. They loved him and so they loved me. I felt unconditionally loved by every one of them, no judgements made and acceptance in all things. The only proviso was that I shouldn't hurt their brother, but that was, as I was soon deeply in love with him, unlikely. I loved him. His laugh, his madness, his humour, his cock, his way of making everyone feel special. He was unlike anyone I had ever known and I felt blessed and happy for the first time in my life I think. We drank too much, smoked too much, laughed and fucked, but never too much! There could never be too much of those! It was blissful and hilarious, it was full of laughter and cum and validation, of trips to Brighton, of big Sunday roasts with any number of people who might turn up, or who might have been invited by Rod, with his beer goggles on and his way of making people agree, *"Kaff won't mind!"*, down the Royal Oak on Sunday lunchtime. Down the club in the evenings at the weekend, maybe on to The Pigeons on the Romford Road. Then home, sex or not depending how pissed we were....on and on through the fag end of summer 1980, Brighton for my birthday, *'Ashes to Ashes', 'The Winner Takes it All', 'Oops Upside Your Head'* and over and over, *'Give Me The Night'* – these were the soundtrack of my love. Della Reese, Alma Cogan, Mel Tormé...new voices, new sounds, slow dancing in the lounge in the dark; hiding out in the attic with bottles of gin and making love in silence to see if we could. A whole spinning, swirling world of feeling and emotions that I had never known and I knew this would last for ever. And in a funny way it has – I am still wearing a ring he bought me in Romford market 35 years ago; we split up after four years, didn't meet again for another twenty five, when he was dying; dying, but still working the room like a pro. We met up again in Brighton, my new man and me, and Rod was nothing but generous and warm and welcoming to him. It was his 65th birthday and we had been lucky enough to have been in Cornwall and I had arranged to go and see him on the way home. It was wonderful, sad, joyful – it was like the intervening 25 years hadn't happened. He was still the same man I had loved, still love and he resides in my heart. He held me to his hairy chest, to his heart, and in that moment all was forgiven. *"I'll come to France to see you both,"* he said, but he barely had breath to get to the kitchen – we both knew this would never be, but the pretence was less painful. The last thing he said, mouthed to me, and did with his fingers as he waved us off, from the balcony on the top floor, was '1.4.3.', 'I', 'LOVE' 'YOU', the little secret gesture we'd had, made with our fingers, exchanged surreptitiously, secretly in our love, at parties, across rooms, in straight pubs, over dinners in restaurants. He made it with the hand not holding the railing, and keeping him on his feet, and I gestured back; a simple but profound gesture signifying that we loved, we had loved and we always will. He's gone now – he died on August 8th 2008, 30 years to the day we met, but he is here in this house and in my heart still.

● ● ●

Our love was perfect. I thought so, anyway. We lived in Audley Gardens, Ilford, near Seven Sisters tube – me, Rod, Kath, Keith (then Neil), Kath's two boys, Troy who rented the attic and various dossers and waifs and strays. A small digression here, but a tale worth telling...

Troy was a PROPER gay boy, all skin tight jeans and blonde streaked hair. He wore blouses and always drank bloody Marys, large, with an olive. He lived up in the attic and we rarely saw him (although Rod had shagged him one night – or tried to but they apparently just laughed themselves to sleep instead) and he was always so sweet and gentle. BUT, if you crossed him, or hurt one of his 'chickens', (us) he was fierce, Mama, FIERCE! Anyway, this particular night, we were in a cab, heading for the club, and we saw Troy walking along Leytonstone High Road, Selina's bound too. At the crossroads at the Thatched House, a car pulled up at the red lights, just as Troy minced up to the junction.

"OY!" said a yoof, hanging out of the open back window. "ARE YOU A POOF?"

Without missing a beat, Troy turned on his Cuban heel and marched straight over to the car. We watched, in fascinated horror. He was a big bloke, Troy was, but there was a car full of THEM. Rod had his hand on the cab door handle ready to pitch in, when we heard:

"I'm sorry, love. Are you addressing moi?"

"Yeah. I said 'ARE YOU A NANCY BOY POOFTER?"

Troy - and I swear this is true – leant over, ignoring the cars that were now beeping as the lights had changed and leant into the car and said,

"Are you?"

"Wot, a poofter? No I fucking ain't!"

"Well, then," said Troy, through the open window and right into the face of the driver: "FUCK OFF and stop wasting my time". And just turned away, waved at the cars, swept his hair in a manner insouciant, and minced off up the road.

We roared, and applauded through our open cab window, and he waved, and yelled, "I'll have a double, and don't forget the fucking olive!"

So, that was Troy, all camp, fierce, beautiful and the lodger in the loft. And the rest of the house was just as exciting to a boy like me, hurting still, needing companions, friends and a lover. All of which I seemed to have. All at once

How Kath managed to cater for us all remains a mystery to me (although the dinner she constructed for us this last Christmas was like alchemy so I guess she was just born to it) but the house ran on chaos and love. And I was happier than I could have thought possible.

Lucky Mr. Lucky!

After the debacle of the Traveller's Unit, I'd been shunted off down into the depths of the docks. Like it was MY fucking fault! Shoulda done your research Mr. L.E.A. Man….. Anyway, the school was an old Victorian edifice, interior walls painted green with tiled dado rails – more like an asylum than a school, and so it proved to be. Again, I was introduced to my class – not, and helped by the other teachers – not, and so I faced what is now known as Y4, sitting stony faced and sullen at the prospect of yet another teacher.

"This is your new teacher, class. It will be nice to have a permanent teacher after so many supply teachers, won't it?"

Grunts.

"Wossis name?"

This is Mr….Erm….. I don't know actually. Nobody's actually told me…"

And so began a very short residency at Prince Edward Primary. The head had his office tucked away out of reach of anything that might be threatening, such as a child, but at break I went to find him and to ask: *"Can you tell me a little about the class, please? They seem rather ….disengaged…"* (I didn't actually say 'disengaged' as I only recently learned this word, but I said something similar).

"Oh, yes. They are. Fed up of a constant train of supply teachers. Doesn't give much stability, do you see? You're in charge of Art. Jolly good."

"I am? No one said." In fact, nobody had said ANYTHING, other than the address and a start date. I looked around the school, in the corridors, in the hall – nothing. Just blank walls. No wonder the kids were so blank. I was on a mission to get Art work up, justify my post this time. But I hadn't reckoned on Class 4 and their complete unwillingness to do any work whatsoever, nor answer questions, write anything down or listen. It was like shoving shit uphill.

No one listened, to me or each other. It was like being in a zoo, or a bad movie which had no end. The days passed in a maelstrom of noise and hurled objects that I was powerless to stop. I didn't have the tools in my tool box for this – I'd had one year's experience in a classroom to date and clearly my training at Balls Park (BALLS PARK!!! HAHAHAAA) didn't cover this bit: what to do when faced with a room full of fucking morons whose only *raison d'etre* was to be each noisier, more destructive and more vile than everyone else. I look back on this episode in my professional life with a kind of wonder….how could such a class of children ever have been allowed to deteriorate to that level of disinterest and fury? Looking back, those kids weren't to blame - it sounded like, that for whatever reason, they'd been abandoned, one supply teacher after another, no consistency, no discipline that was ongoing….they were lost. If it had been later in my career, I know I could have rescued them – I had the skills and would have brought them back. This was 1981 – they would be in their early 40s now – what kind of lives did they have? How did they fare in the world of Thatcherism and greed – getting 'decent jobs, for decent people'? They probably were decent people, had they been schooled well, and I would have been the man to do it, I'd like to think. But, this was '81, I was 25 – and shit scared of them, if I'm being honest. They were like the baying mob in the Coliseum or something. So, coming from a place of fear, I was an easy target, both figuratively and literally. No one listened. The lesson plans I had assiduously prepared, to 'engage' them, to 'stimulate' them, to 'include' them all went to shit. Never got off the ground. Much like my plans to turn the school into a wonderland of art and creativity. Nobody, and that includes the other staff, was in the least interested. There was no paper, no materials, no equipment and no interest. I suppose the bleakness of the school suited the bleakness of their ambition and they produced NOTHING, or nothing that I would consider worth displaying. It was very dispiriting, day after day, getting nowhere.

It didn't go on for long however. It was on a Friday, date unknown, that the camel's back got broken. It was an art lesson (I was nothing if not optimistic) and suddenly a boy pulled out a penknife and started yelling about who he was going to stab first. I wasn't really prepared for this – this wasn't in the College curriculum – so I asked him to give me the knife. He called me a *'Nancy Cunt'* (what a strange insult!) and got under a desk. Nothing would persuade him to come out, so I gave up trying. And as I returned to my desk, from behind me, a jam jar that we'd been using for water for painting, came flying through the air, past my head and smashed against the tiled wall surrounding the blackboard. I didn't turn, didn't ask. I just collected my jacket from the chair, shook off the shards of broken jam jar, picked up my briefcase, and turned to leave the room, with its smashed glass and boy with a knife, who said, "*Where you goin'?*"

"*Somewhere I'll hopefully never have to see YOU again. You little…er..CUNT.*"

I then went along the bleak green corridors to the head's office, and said:

"I'm leaving. Now. Goodbye."

"You can't do that! What about the children? What about your contract? You can't just LEAVE….!"

"I didn't sign one - I was just dumped here. And as for the children – your problem. Good luck and watch out for the little shit with the knife."

And I walked out, walked away and left Education, with its ignorant rules and massive failings, behind.

Coo! How brave! How militant! How…..unemployed….

As ever, the family was supportive, with Rod threatening to go and find the little bastard and give "'im a good 'idin'", but I said that wasn't necessary. What WAS necessary was finding some work so I could pay my way in the house. I wasn't good at much else, when you came down to it. Want me to express myself in modern dance, maybe in a blue sack, anybody? No, I thought not, so I was going to have to get out into the real world. I got a job selling insurance, which was commission only and really really shit. I was rubbish at it anyway:

"Oh good evening Madam, I'm from….."

"Fuck off".

"Oh, OK, then. Sorry to have bothered you"

That was pretty much how it went. I even, (shame on me; I can't believe the depths I sank to at times) went round to Julie's, who had got herself a new flat, and after I'd rung to say *'Oh! Hi! How ARE you?"* she invited me round for tea. Alright, dinner…..

Anyway, she made no mention of me turning up with my briefcase, and we had a nice, if a little awkward, meal and then I said, *"Would you be interested in buying any life insurance?"*

Scumbag, honestly. I really don't blame her for chucking me out. Actually, that was the last time I saw her for a few years, the next time being in less pleasant circumstances.

Well that didn't last long. I'd walked about a billion miles and sold….nothing. Nante.

So.....

A milk round! Yes. Brilliant. Except the excitement of chugging across Hackney Marshes at 04.00 a.m. in a milk float with no doors, at 4 mph, in the winter, pretty soon wore off. As did finding none of the bastard lifts working in the tower blocks; after traipsing up 15 floors with two pints of milk – **Leyton Dairies! We pride ourselves on that personal touch! Milk with a smile!** – only to find Gladys wanted an extra pint / a yoghurt / some orange juice today. Down 15 floors. Up 15 floors. *"Oh, could I have two bottles of Juice. I forgot my Maisie's coming today and she's a bit partial. Thanks, love."* It was very hard not to stick the yoghurt up her arse, but...Milk with a smile! This happened so often, in the end there was nearly fights to see who would 'do the flats'. Not me, obvs. as I was much too genteel. I just waited politely until breakfast and the awesome smoked salmon and cream cheese bagels in Ridley Road market, which signalled the end of the round. Then back to base to count the thousands of coins that all the old girls had paid with. We did, quite often, plan to stage a robbery where one of us would get beaten up and the money bag nicked, but as it always seemed to be me that got chosen to be duffed up, I refused.

Anyway, this career didn't last long. Too cold, too tiring, too butch.

My next wheeze to was to join a security firm, partly because it was just down the road and I could walk to work, but also because I assumed all you had to do was sit in a van all day. I went along, took a 'test', basically to determine that I could spell my own name and address, got hired the same day, start on Monday...

Well, I hadn't seen the men who worked for PPS, and if I had I might not have applied. How gorillas and Piltdown men had learned to drive was a marvellous thing, and I soon found myself amongst a company of men that I thought only existed in Dickens or in Hogarth's paintings. I had led a sheltered life, as you know, and my only experience of adult men had been the fey sort, or at least those who'd been to RADA or had jazz hands. These men seemed to be an entirely different species altogether. Nobody talked, they all shouted, and if you would read this next part in, say a Bob Hoskins, or a Danny Dyer voice, it will help you to get a better understanding of how I, this tender homosexual who like to 'sa *'Hulls sky, hullo clouds'* and skip about like a gurl', found myself marooned on the Planet of the Apes.

Monday. 08.30.

"Ere's yer uniform. Get it on and get dahn the mess room."

• • •

"Erm…yes…er..Sir."

"Dahnt call me fackin, Sir, it aint the fackin army."

"erm, no Sir. I mean, Mr. erm Mr. Boss, thankyou. Erm, where is the mess room?"

"Dahn the back. Go on, get a fackin move on. You're out on Van 651 at 9.00."

"But I haven't had any training, or anything. What do I do?"

"Oh fer FACK'S sake. ASK, ask the uvva blokes. Train on the job. Now, fack off. I'm busy."

And that, dear reader, was my 'induction'.

I opened the brown paper sack, and there lay……my uniform. Nylon. Zip up jacket, nylon trousers. And it was cerise. I kid you not. FUCKING CERISE! How could I go out in THAT? What if anyone saw me? I would just DIE! But, sensing they weren't going to let me chose my own colour scheme, I began to put on the uniform, which actually still smelled of its former occupant. Ewwww. All stale sweat and fags. I was beginning to regret my snap decision and not to have gone a wee bit further afield in my job search…..

Anyway, suited and booted, I went back through the building and found the Mess Room. 'Mess' describes it perfectly. Full of tatty old chairs, empty take away cartons, overflowing ashtrays, empty sweet wrappers, coke cans and half-drunk cups of tea and coffee, littered the tables and windowsills. It smelled of fags and farts and well, BLOKES.

"Aye Aye! Ooze this then?" somebody said, as I appeared in the doorway. *"A new one!"*

"Oh, hello". (Lower your voice, you pratt). *"Oh Hello. I'm"*…..and in the beat before I said it, I knew I would be committing social suicide, right there on the steps of the Mess Room, if I admitted to being called Nigel. I might as well have said 'Tarquin' or 'Rupert'…..*"Steve. Yeah. Steve. Erm…Oright?"*

"Yeah, oright. Wotcher Steve. Come in. Acshally, don't. We ain't got time for a cuppa, cos we're aht at nine an iss five to nah. Fack me, we'll be late"

And he grabbed my arm and led me towards the van, opened the door and flung me in and set the locks. I had no idea what to do! I just sat there in the semi darkness, and waited for the next thing to happen, which was the radio crackled into life, a voice said 'Copy 651', and we were off. Fuck knows where or why. But we were off. And, oh God, it was BOILING!

Not much to report on this really. Lots of sweating, lots of misogyny and lots of swearing. I thought I was bad until I heard one of the blokes (for blokes they are, not chaps, nor fellows) describing a car accident he'd seen on the way to work:

"FACK ME! YOU SHOULDA FACKIN SEEN THA FACKIN MOTA! FACK! IT WAS FACKIN FACKED TA FACK".

10/10 for completely destroying the language. Well done, that man! I mean, Bloke.

My work days consisted of either driving the van (cool), being the 'runner' (not so cool) or 'back man' (shit). The driver part is self-explanatory – the firm covered all of greater London, and I got to know the city and outskirts extremely well. PLUS, if we were late for base, or sometimes for lunch, we could call up the old Bill and they'd 'see us in'. This meant they'd turn up, stick their blue lights on and we could follow them down the bus lanes, thus saving valuable sandwich time. Whilst driving, it gave my 'runner' ample opportunity to ogle and all the passing women, go PHWOAR a lot, ask me *'if I fancied a bit of that'* and *'what I thought of her tits'*. When he got out to collect or deliver bags (cash, cheques, wages, coin) there was ample opportunity to find out, from passing females, whether if he *"met her at the Pawnbrokers, would she kiss me under the balls?"* Invariably they said *'no'*, or *'fuck off you pervy bastard'*, which usually served to inflame his ardour further, so he could do more PHWOARing, a bit of whistling, and inform her that she must be gagging for it. This went on ad nauseam, and was one of the downsides of driving – you couldn't get away from it. He'd do the bag dump, get back in, say *"OK, Sarf Ken next, Cahncil Offices"* (like I didn't know). *"Did you see the tits on that? Bet she's got a fanny like the Blackwall Tahnnel."* I hadn't actually seen the 'tits on that'; well, I HAD, but only as an observation. But I HAD seen the rather marvellous bulge in the trousers of the man leaning up against the wall of the bank. But I was guessing he didn't want to compare notes, so....I drove on. To Sarf Ken.

Being in the midst of all this macho shit was really really wearing. I was clearly the only gay in the village (though I reckon there was one, if pushed......) and I really didn't fit it. I couldn't stand the mess, the fucking and cunting, the farting and the noise. Was this Class 4, projected into the future? And most offensive was the way they spoke to, and of, women. I'm not naive – I know this goes on, and was far worse back in the '80s and I supposed I was living in a microcosm swirling with testosterone, but, please.....boys.....nobody want to kiss your balls, or suck you off (well, I might, but that's in another universe) or want to let you *'take them up the alley'*. Really they don't. You all stink of fags and sweat, and the uniform...well, cerise doesn't really do it for the laydees. So shut the fuck up and get on with your work.

Sarf Ken done, lunch, the rest of the West End (witnessed a crash on Marble Arch roundabout between a white van and a mini. The mini contained, FIVE NUNS, who all got out and started shouting at the white van man. Sadly, the lights changed and I had to drive on, so I never witnessed the end....I hope they were gentle with him) then back to base, coin check, bag count, then home. That was my day. Then into the furry arms of my Rod, who smelled of sawdust and love.

If you were a 'runner', you were in and out of the van all day, taking bags put into the safe by the 'back man' into banks, shops, offices and chucking full ones into the safe if it was a collection. It gave me a bit of ogling time of my own, but I didn't share it with my driver, for obvious reasons.

Being the 'back man' was the worst of the three – long shifts locked in the back, hot and itchy, chuckin' bags out, pullin' bags in. At least there was a chance to read a bit between drops and if it rained, you stayed dry, but claustrophobics need not apply. I still have a damaged first finger on my left (chord playing!!) hand from where it got it trapped in the safe one day as I slammed it shut, and someone left a Post-It inside the window of the van, with 'IS BRAY GAY?' on it. But other than that, being the 'back man' was dry, hot and dark – the small thickly reinforced windows didn't let in much light and there is steel partition between the cab and the back, in case anyone got in. And so the days passed....I DID get interviewed by the police about the Brinks-Matt robbery, which happened in November '83 but nothing much else to say really. Except – if you haven't eaten your sandwiches, on Christmas Eve, sitting in a van, literally sitting, on half a million pounds of gold bullion, as it races through London, flanked by police cars, with their blue light flashing, then you have missed out on a rare thrill.

For some reason, in about '82, Rod and Kath decided to sell Audley Gardens and to go their separate ways, house wise. She had a new chap, Rod had me, and all seemed to be stable and maybe sharing a house was now a bit wrong. A bit Famous Five – nobody could really shag when they wanted, and had to be careful of the noise etc. We'd had some FABLIUS times there – Gill, to whom I had come out long since, came up one Christmas and she, a leather queen called Phil (who frankly couldn't really pull it off; think Pinocchio in chaps) and I found some poppers (google it, people!) and went...wait for it....behind the Christmas Tree to have a sniff, and then all fell out on the floor, pushing over the tree and fusing the lights as we fell. Well, WE thought it was funny....I still laugh at the time there was a bees nest in the wall and Keith went up onto the conservatory roof and Rod took the ladder away; the bees attacked Keith and he fell through the roof. Mick (it was MILLSY, Chris, not Milly!) who was painting in the lounge, kicked over a large tin of white gloss paint on the brown shag pile rug and fell in it himself trying to scrape it up.....My how we laughed! Neil poured a large tin of spaghetti hoops over the top of the shower on to Kath and then hid all the towels.....jolly japes. Many more in my head and memories made. But, it became time to move on and so the house was sold; Kath and Neil went one way, Rod and I, another, and so endeth a chapter. One for which I will always be grateful to have shared – the happiest time of my life to date.

CHAPTER THREE.

FOUR BOYFRIENDS AND A FUNERAL.

In which our hero gets 'tempest tossed and sore afflicted' and the lights go out.

'Ghosts'.

by Japan. No5. April 4th. 1982.

Just when I thought it was going to be alright – haunted by ghosts of failure.

~ ~ ~

Kath and Neil only moved down the road, the other side of the station – a bijou little maisonette. They must've made a packet on the house as the new gaff was about a quarter of the size, notwithstanding sharing the profit with Rod.

We, on the other hand, were waiting for a flat on Cranbrook road to be finished – a very des.res. And now worth a mint. Whilst we waited, we had a little flat in Seymour Gardens, still just off Cranbrook, so still a *bit* posh, and that is when things began to go wrong. Not that I acknowledged this – this was my Forever Love and so I would not allow any cracks to appear, any enemies breach the turrets. There HAD been an incident while we were still at Audley Gardens, somehow all ending up in bed, but I thought once we'd moved, I could say it was a blip, an experiment and it would have no impact on our lives. Oh, you silly silly boy.

Somehow, I had regained contact with Tony; I have no memory of how – I MUST have contacted him as he wouldn't have had my number, so ......anyway, he had invited us to a party, a house warming at his new pad in Whitechapel and very beautiful it was, paid for no doubt by the luxuriant garden of marijuana, and his drugs trade. It was just as the area was up and coming and he'd been a clever boy and bought in.

The party was very good, I think. Plenty of food, plenty of people, plenty of drink. After the crowds had gone, we all settled down in the snug, big plumptious settees and pouffes, (both kinds) and as we talked and drank, I noticed that Rod's stockinged foot was rubbing Tony's groin, as he sat there, legs spread wide, drinking wine. I only dimly registered this, as I was seriously pissed by then. So much so, that I was sick. Not on Tony's new cream carpets luckily, but Rod said, *"Probably best if you go to bed, eh? You'll be better if you sleep."* (I am, of course, paraphrasing – this was over 30 years ago and I was very drunk; falling over drunk). So, he helped me up the quaint old staircase to the quaint little bedroom and to the quaint little bed, where I fell instantly into a quaint little drunken stupor.

The next bit I have made up, but the bare bones are true, as he told me, after. Rod, with me out of the way, went downstairs and fucked Tony. Had sex with him. Shagged him. Let him touch his beautiful chest. Spread his fucking slutty legs and persuaded my Rod to fuck him.

Actually, it was not as bad, and worse at the same time. What actually had happened was that the 4 or 5 people left had sex, so it 'wasn't personal. Apparently. "It was just sex, it didn't mean anything, babe". And they were drunk. It just happened. And you know what? I accepted it. Because I adored this man, and his funny smile and his knobbly knees and his Jewish patois. That's why. I hated him and I loved him, the first of those feelings being a bit alien and alarming and unwelcome so I pretended I didn't feel it. So, how we ended up in OUR bed, with Tony, in our house, not his, I have no idea. I have this photo, so I didn't imagine it and I do remember that the sex was amazing. (I hope you Googled 'poppers', when I told you to...) but HOW? And more to the point...WHY?

Tony and Me.

The phone rang one day, in the fag end of the moving process, and it was Tony.

"Oh hi. It's Tony. Wondered if you fancied coming over?"

"No. We don't. Thankyou."

"Why? What's happened? What about the other night?"

"That was a mistake. It won't be happening again." And with Tony, it didn't.

"Oh, so YOU'RE the nigger in the woodpile are you?" (I've never been called that before or since!) *"What does Rod think?"*

"The same, of course."

We both knew it to be a blatant lie, but I was NOT having this man's hands, or bits, anywhere near my man again.

Rod knew nothing of this call; I never told him how I had put the kibosh on this..this...thing. Mama lion protecting her own.

"Oh. Well. Shame. He was a good fuck. See you around." OUCH, bastard. But I never did. See him again, I mean. A bit of a sad ending; I actually owed him a debt, he was a player in my story, back in Blackheath when I was but a fledgling, AND he'd taken my virginity you will recall, but...too close, way too close. And I was far too insecure.

So, post Tony, we were moving to our temporary little love nest, while waiting for our proper Forever Home to be finished.

One of the gang, Eddie, a tailor of ecclesiastical robes on Saville Row, known of course as Edie, would often come and stay over at Audley Gardens, (we had 5 bedrooms there – usually full of drunken waifs and strays!) and was always around. A good mate. Singularly unattractive - I mean, just like a sister and never in the sexual orbit – and never a threat. Until.......the flat in Seymour gardens was a one bedroomed flat, so one drunken night, Rod decided it would be a good idea if we all slept on the floor in the lounge. What the hell...?? But, I always, always wanted to please him, to soothe this hurt in him, so I agreed.

The next thing I know, we're having sex. Me, Rod and Edie. It was the last thing I expected to be honest. Edie? EDIE? It was like shagging your sister.....a bit weird, I can tell you, yet.....always led by my cock and the heat of the moment. I'll spare you the details....

• • •

After, Rod said it didn't matter – he was a friend, it was just a bit of harmless fun, and anyway, Edie didn't get much so it was like a nice thing to do. What? I'm a charity now? But as always, I acquiesced and tried not to let it matter.

You can see where this is going can't you? I began to as well, as more and more often when we went out, I would get the *'He's nice. Him over there. Do you want to bring him home?'* routine and as often as not, we did. Hugh, who we picked up in The London Apprentice (and who Rod sucked off in the back seat whilst I drove drunkenly home, my heart racing from the amyl nitrate filling the car) became a regular, although that fizzled out when I accidently did a poo on his carpet. I won't go into details – I'm sure your imaginations are fertile enough to make a good guess why. There were others – friends from the club, strangers from toilets, often from the cottage on the corner of Dames Road in Wanstead. I'd sit and wait in the car while Rod would disappear into the inky depths of the toilet and emerge with some random stranger, who could have been anyone in the dark and, like some deranged getaway driver, I'd drive us home, while they noshed each other's faces and cocks in the back seat.

I hated it. I hated it with every fibre of my being. So why, you dozy twat, did you do it? Is that the question forming on your lips? 'Because I loved him', comes the pathetic reply. Because I was scared that if I refused, he would leave me. That if I didn't offer myself up, that he would find someone who would. You know: the usual cry of the abused spouse.

Looking back down the years, given what I had (have) always wanted from my life, i.e. a man who would love ME, and only ME, FOR me, and exclusively ME, a break up with Rod was inevitable. I have still not come to understand what drove him, what made him desire others, at the expense of his lovers, and I was by no means the first – I met several at his funeral - and even when witness to the pain it brought. Was he a sex addict (a real one I mean) or did he just like cock? He clearly wasn't satisfied with mine and as this situation progressed, and I granted more and more permission, it became clear that our definitions of 'love' were somewhat different. It became painful. It became humiliating – I hated to see the man I adored with his cock up someone else's arse, to see some stranger's mouth around his dick, on his chest, on his mouth. *"For fuck's sake! It's only sex!"* was becoming an argument that was less and less acceptable. Every time it happened, a little piece of me broke off and those pieces, over time, floated away and coalesced into another person, an observer, someone who watched proceedings as if it were a porn film. Certainly I was physically involved – my cock was sucked, I had a cock, his and the Stranger's, in my mouth and ass, but it was like I was just in the room, in the corner, watching someone else's heaving buttocks, hearing someone else's panting and groaning as we all came, one after the other. I, the real me, the man who thought his travels were done and was to rest in the encircling arms of this funny, gentle man for ever, was diminishing, was becoming smaller, disappointed, lost again. This was NOT in the script. This was NOT supposed to happen. AGAIN.

Talking about it proved fruitless. He'd either say (resentfully, angrily) *'OK, I won't do it again'* or we'd have the conversation based around; *"but I DO love you. I fuck you, don't I?"* (That bit was meant to be a joke, but in the light of things, not a very good one). *"I don't want anyone else. We've bought a house together....it's just that...you know...."* And then the argument about open relationships and how, if I REALLY loved him, I would *know* it didn't matter, that it was 'only sex'. And, maybe for him, that was the truth. I know, knew of then, people whose relationships thrived on such an arrangement (and many which did not – jealousies, insecurities, one – upmanship, all played out in the embers of the dying light, which was always ignored, justified, until it was too late, leaving the two people to be as 'open' as they liked, as they were now single again). But it didn't work for me. Not then and not years later, as I bravely tried to save the remnants of my imploding marriage. But that's a later story.

Right now, in the summer of 1984, with Frankie, Moyet, Somerville and Wham! and Elton marking the going down of my sun, I was finding my position unbearable, painful beyond words. What was wrong with *ME*? A question always answered with *'nothing, babe. Honest'*, but it never served. I felt ugly, unsexy, unimportant and...well, scared. How can I keep doing this? Answer: I can't. How can I leave him? Answer: I can't. I DID need a *'Love Resurrection'* but I didn't know how. I did *'Let the sun go down on me'*, in my heart, as it shrank, just as I let some random stranger go down on me in my bed, trying to please, and failing to feel.

The end came quite suddenly, in the same year. On the surface all was well. Meeting after work, in the Jolly Sailor in Barking, Rod and his brother Tony smelling of sawdust, me smelling of failure; dinner, bit of telly; getting ready to go to Selina's (which was much safer as we'd had everyone there, between us) and then the dread of, *"Shall we go via Dames Road? Fancy it?"* What was I supposed to say? Not agreeing led to sullen argumentative days; agreeing led to a quick fuck and my sunny Rod, back to normal. It was, looking back at the pattern, like a fix for him. And I was aiding and abetting his addiction. Buying his drug.

● ● ●

Amongst all of this sorrow / joy, there was one other very important, pivotal event that occurred and changed forever the dynamics of the relationship with my family. We had a brand new home, a mezuzah on our door (which belonged to the wonderful old Jewish couple upstairs, but they didn't mind it we rubbed it) to bless our home. I know I didn't technically own it – the mortgage was in Rod's name, he had put down the deposit – but as far as I was concerned, it was MY first ever nest, and I intended to feather it beautifully. We did it up, and the first months were as good as they could possibly have been, him fucking other men aside....

I'd not heard much from down West lately. Gill had been up at Christmas and she'd kept in regular touch but as far as Ma and Pa knew, I had moved and was sharing a nice new house in a 'respectable part' of London, as indeed I was, except for the omission of the fact that my flatmate shagged me, and was my lover. As in BOYFRIEND. This status quo seemed to suit everyone, on a need to know basis. Chris had by now, met the love of his life, and he and Vince were getting a place together. He seemed calmer and happier and by default, we didn't see so much of each other and my life (apart from the hated aforementioned moments of sharing) was even, and even ...fun!

One evening, November 1983, the phone rang.

"It's me."

"Hi, Gill! OK!?"

"Erm....no......." and she burst in to tears. I finally manage to get that the shit had hit the fan – like, elephant sized turds.....Dad and she had gone for a walk in to town. So far so normal. Then, *a propos* of nothing, staring straight ahead (I had all the minutiae from a very shocked sister) said:

"Is Nigel a homosexual?"

She said the blood just drained from her heart and in response all she could answer was,

"You'd better ask HIM."

"That's what I thought," was all he replied.

What happened next, and over the next few days is unknown to me other than what has been reported.

The usual silence (aka. Didn't get my own way; wasn't considered first; sulk) followed until a few days later, by all accounts he and Mum having a stand up row, right there, in the middle of Newquay High Street. Well, when I say 'row', I mean he yelled and screamed and ranted at her (Odd, given he wanted to keep this monstrous fact a secret) saying it was all her fault for bringing me up 'like a girl' Did he have a point? I was effeminate, at least in HIS eyes; I DID 'sa *hullo clouds, hullo sky*", a lot and skip about '*like a gurl*', not only at school, which he hadn't seen, but also at home, which he did. I did, latterly swan about in a fur coat – but that was just teenagerism, hippiness....

Nobody makes you queer, Dad, no matter what you think. There IS no blame here. Mum, of course, (foolishly, but I imagine, in her fury, brought out by this public shaming) said that she had known for years; Gill knew, Sandra knew; we had had one to stay in our house! At which point, he went nuclear.

Now, at the point (in my naive imagination) where I thought that now, maybe as it was 'official', when I wanted, needed, reassurance and support, he would take me to one side, man to man and say something along the lines of: *"Well, Son. I respect you for not telling me as you knew I might be upset, but I am not. I am proud of you, proud of what you have achieved – a teacher! A teacher in the family! Someone who went to College and was even asked to go to Cambridge! Thank you for considering my feelings and not wanting to cause me dismay – but how could I? You are a wonderful son and a good human being who will do good things in the world"*

I wrote to them, my parents, expressing my gratitude for their understanding, acceptance and to thank them for giving me the life I had. What he actually did, was to write me a letter in return, from which I quote, and the power of which causes me such sorrow, such hurt, even nearly 30 years after he wrote it:

'Yours to hand, I would imagine that it must be the standard letter as supplied in text form by The Shit Shovers Union to placate parents who have just discovered that their son is a fully paid up member, and having made all the appropriate platitudes to explain away the bestial, disgusting depravity of abusing your body and mind, that all will be forgiven and the whole thing will be swept under the carpet and we all go on with our normal lives as if nothing had happened.

Well, it is not like that for us (I doubt Mum had anything to do with this, and he was NOT speaking for her at all). *We are going to make you bear some of the weight of the cross you have made us carry, what you have done to your parents. You have DESTROYED the two people who gave you life and have loved you fiercely all the years and now all this love has gone......after much soul searching I have decided to leave this house, to leave her here. I CURSE you for what you are doing to yourself and what you have done to your parents and I hope this letter will stop you from engaging in these bestial acts, and that you may hear our cry of anguish and might say to yourself 'I once had a mother and father'. I know we shall ask ourselves: 'not did where we go wrong, but how could you do this to us'*

Do not phone.

Yours in blood only.

Dad.'

I have left out the more unpleasant parts.

This dear reader was, as you can imagine, NOT what I wanted to hear. Shock. Dismay. Hurt. Anger. You're my DAD, my FATHER, and here you are, AGAIN, giving me no support, no love, no feelings that it will all be OK. How many more times will you do this to me?

As you were dying, I came to you and told you I understood, that I forgave you. But I think I was lying. I could forgive you for what you did to me, but never for what you did to Gill, to Sandra, to my Mother. All of us, damaged due to your intransigence, your petty spite and grudges. What your letter did, in fact, after I'd laughed it off, bravado flying like rain, was to set up, deep inside me a feeling of shame – not for being gay, exactly but for the fact of my very *being* so was causing so much pain and upset, sadness and hurt.

I AM GAY.

I AM A GAY MAN.

I AM A GOOD PERSON.

I HAVE WORTH.

I HAVE LOVE AND GIVE IT FREELY.

I AM A GAY MAN.

It took me years, years, to be able to say this, to recover from the poisoning administered to me by my Father, who not only actively poured hated and disgust upon me, but also didn't stand by me, when I was telling my truth, when I most needed love and support and acceptance. I DIDN'T smash those windows, and when I needed you again, here, at this most pivotal moment of my life, you weren't there.

I had been in London for years, as you know, fucking and shopping, as the play said, (only without those coy asterisks) - for love, had found love, had lived a happy life, lived a sad life, just like everyone else, I have had a 'normal' life. Successful in parts, tragic in others. I've been Mr. Lucky more often than not, but had some grim intervals. I have worked to keep food on the tables in the various places I have found myself. I have contributed, as a person, as a lover and as a friend, as an educator and supporter. So you dare. You fucking DARE judge me as a bad person, someone you hardly know, as you had never bothered to ask, simply because of who I share a bed with.

Ach, enough. This rant, this interminable rant we poofters have against our parents! Enough already. He's made up his mind (in a rather melodramatic fashion in my view!) and **that**, as we all know, was **that.**

What happened next, as I have heard from the other, more rational members of the family strays in to Farce. He instantly revoked his memberships of all his clubs at the Legion – including his beloved Euchre team, because apparently *"everyone would know"*. Sorry? How exactly? You wouldn't breathe a word and I'm in London..! *("Trevor,"* said my indomitable Mother, *"Joe and Brian are both gay! If you can't tell, then I can. They're not leaving the team, are they? It's private."* Maybe THAT'S why he left – in case he caught it from *them…*

He screamed and raved at my poor mother for 'making me a queer bastard', for not bringing me up properly, for treating me like a girl, for, for….for EVERYTHING. None of it, obviously, was his fault – not that there WAS any 'fault' to be had.

He shut all the curtains, wouldn't go out, refused to answer the phone or the door, refused to eat. In the end, worried about what was going on in the house, my brother and Gill got the priest from St. Mary's (the one who absolved Mary from her shagging sins) but, after shouting through the letter box (please, try to get a mental picture of this!), the door opened and Dad, whiskered, unshaven and filthy, opened the door, stared at the three of them, and then BLAM! Slammed the door in the priest's face. There wasn't really much to add to that really, so they all went home.

My indomitable Auntie Gwen, who'd I'd known all me life, had come down to try to help with the crisis – I am assuming Mum must've phoned and told her. When he announced: *"I'd rather he was a spastic in a wheelchair, than one of*

THEM," she gave him *SUCH* a bollocking, I think he lost the power of speech. At any rate, he never spoke a word for days, just drifted from room to room, crying and wailing.

One GOOD thing that came from this lunacy was that my Mother had a 'FUCK YOU!' moment and announced that she was going up to London – that I was still her son and she wanted to see me. So she did! Excellent! Rod fell in love with her, she was instantly adopted, a feeling she found quite confusing – hugging? Touching? All a bit alien, but you could tell she loved it. Everyone was kind to her, and with her – they knew of the terrible, punishing time she'd had and she blossomed, flowered in the warmth of these people.

We took her to Brighton - there was a huge party, and we booked her in to a hotel, all posh like and she was treated like a queen. By all the queens.

My Mum, with Billy and Jan.

Billy and Jan loved her; the total acceptance of her, and her son by all of these people, some of whom she had met only hours before, was puzzling to her, but was a clue that there could be a different kind of life, peopled with kindness and joy.

My Mother with Uncle Billy, in Brighton!

She came up to see me several times over this period, the one during which I was *persona non gratis*. On one occasion, and this dates it to Spring, '83, I made her sit and listen to the whole of Pink Floyd's *'The Final Cut'*, really loud....I think it to do with sharing something important to ME with HER. Anyway, after her ears had stopped bleeding, she just said: *"That was nice, dear"*. I felt warm.

It was a strange set up really – he would, wordlessly drive her to the station, when she was taking a trip to 'That Den of Vice', and then meet her from the train on her return. He never once asked her anything – did she have nice time, who did she meet, and, worst and unkindest cut of all, how I was. I had simply ceased to exist. I think SHE saw it as a blessed release.....away from the oppressive silence of her life, her small world. She came to a place of laughter, of fun, of 'being allowed' to spend time with people who asked her questions, showed an interest and made her smile. And I am certain, though deep down I'm sure she would have wished it otherwise, it gave her peace to see that I was safe, I was happy and was loved.

Unfortunately, things were not what they seemed...

As far as the famerly was concerned, all was well. Our new flat was ready, we'd moved in in early March I think. We bought furniture and lamps, beds and cutlery. But my joy was lost – I knew my new home would be spoiled soon enough. And it was.

My fault in a kind of way. It was a Saturday, we went to the club and there was some fresh meat in! Look chaps....someone you haven't had! Kenny. Wee Kenny from Belfast, with his spiky hair and £300 jacket. Like flies round shit, they were. Most odd, but Rod had ordered a cab. Kenny was the belle of the ball and at 11, someone said there was party back at somebody's flat. But strangely, Rod decided he wanted to go home early so Kenny asked *me* to go with him. It was only up the High Road, so I thought I'd tag along, have a bevvy and then head off. To home. Where my Rod would be, alone. Waiting for me. Just me.

Somehow, however, I ended copping off with Kenny. What alchemy was this? He was a twink! A twinky twink, ten years my junior and hairless apart from his Limahl hairdo. What was I thinking? To this day, I don't know. Anyway, we went. Back. To. My. Flat. The one with Rod in it. The demon drink I suppose – but there were far more shaggable people at the party so WHY him, and why, oh WHY did I decide to take him back to my place? Was I bringing a pressy home to Daddy? Like the mouse or headless vole the cat lays at your feet? Or – GASP! - had some unknown signal passed between him and Rod, so that Kenny was

ENGINEERING this? To be brought back to the place where the one he REALLY fancied was, all naked and in bed....Did I WANT to get caught and bring it all to a head? I don't know. What I DO know is that we got back to Cranbrook Road, I opened the front door and got half way down the hall and I chickened out; the jury is out here, as years later, when I asked Rod WHY he did what he then after this night, his version of what he heard is different from mine and from my motives that night – which is why his actions were so utterly utterly devastating later, as I believed I HAD done the right thing.... Sort of.

I remember (as far as anyone can, years later and pissed then) saying: *"No, look, we can't do this. My boyfriend is here. You'll have to go."* Rod insists the pronoun was *"we'll"*. It doesn't alter the fact that *apparently* I WAS going to have sex with Kenny, though God knows why, but I didn't. Rod says I went off with him and came back later in the night. I say I saw him out and went to bed. They're both dead now, so....

The next morning, hung-over and tired, the day started out OK. Rod asked how the party had been, (*"OK, bit boring really."*), who was there (*"Oh the usual crowd. You know."*), did I get home OK, (*"Yeah, I got a cab."*) – all true. Except for the sin of omission. And I didn't know that he'd been awake and heard us come in. And that, dear reader, set him on a path for revenge.

No more was said of it. I thought – hoped – that Kenny was just passing through and he and his silly hair would just have disappeared as suddenly as he'd come and it was done with. Unfortunately, it wasn't and he hadn't.

I need to go backwards a little here, to put all of this into context.

I had travelled down to Plymouth where Gill was living at that time, with the express purpose of telling her about myself. This was long before Rod, but I guess it must have been in the space between leaving Julie and meeting Steve. Eager to validate all the pain I had been the architect of I decided I needed to tell someone, someone meaningful, someone in the family. I was, as most people reading this will either have felt or can guess at how difficult such a thing can be, pretty terrified. The words got stuck somewhere behind my teeth, and it took several beers to prise them open. I don't remember exactly what I said now, but I DO remember we were in her kitchen and she was holding a cucumber. After the words had tumbled out, whatever they were, we both looked at the vegetable and burst out laughing, which on my part eventually turned to sobbing, from relief, an overload of adrenaline and tension – who knows, but there we were, my beloved sister and I, sitting on the kitchen floor, tear – stained with her making improper suggestions as to what she could do with the cucumber.

After this, she became my ally, the one person I could confide in, rest my weary closeted bones. It's likely she suspected, if not knew – the loons and fur coat were a bit of a giveaway – but had been happy not to say anything. Besides, it's not that an easy question to ask, really. It was great though because once my closet door was officially opened, she too could walk through it and meet the creatures that dwelt therein. Of course, Rod adored her, and she him, and she was welcomed in to the family as she were one of their own – an amazing and wondrous thing for her, as she hadn't been exactly supported by her own.

Years before this, boke and living in a hovel with her daughter, she had been forced to make 'Sophie's Choice' and give up her daughter, to her father, Ian – my Dad's Nemesis and Arch Enemy, Spawn of Satan. She simply couldn't afford to feed or clothe her, the house was cold and wet and the choices were few. My parents – well, *him,* and she just did what she was told – were less than supportive of this decision of course, branding Gill as a failure (as if she didn't feel that already, to the pit of her soul) as someone who a) couldn't feed her child and b) as someone who would give her child up. Make up your fucking mind! Which do you want? For me, it was the bravest thing, the most loving thing she could have done for her daughter and one, so it proved, which to be the best outcome for them all – agonising enough and made a thousand times worse by your judgement. (Your sins pile ever higher, you awful man. And with each hurt you pile upon us, the chances of me ever forgiving you drip away, drip, drip..."*Daddy, daddy, you bastard, I'm through!".)*

So, years later, when Rod's family, in all their multi coloured hues of love, opened their collective arms, I could see her healing with every visit, each gaping wound being tenderly closed, with love and laughter and beer. She came fairly often during those few golden years, playing pranks, with Irene, being obscene with Rod, dancing drunk down the club with Millsy, and recovering from those years in the wilderness, and it was of comfort for me too, and the one person who understood the depth and width of my grief when Rod and I parted. She didn't know exactly why, but was wise enough to know it wasn't a decision taken lightly or welcomed in. And of course, it was her loss too.

But, for a time, it was as good as it had ever been – my Gill, my Rod and my overflowing heart all in the room at the same time. I had broken off all contact with my Canadian mistress (though I knew she'd be there if I needed her) and all the bad shit was forgotten.

But then.

But then……Kenny, little twinky Ken, became Rod's trophy – half his age, and full of spunk, literally and figuratively and a perfect way to demonstrate his, Rod's, virility. I'm not sure what it demonstrated to me, after I'd made it (disastrously) clear that it was to be 'ME OR HIM!!!!' and found myself sleeping in the other room, listening to them fucking their brains out, next door, in MY bed, using MY poppers - other than maybe this was going to end badly after all. But what to do? I owned the flat, or half of it, and his family was my family – how could I give them up? I couldn't, I FUCKING WOULDN'T you baldy fucking CUNT. Screw Kenny, screw you. It's MY flat, MY CD player, MY telly and I'm STAYING. That, it seems, was cool with them – they liked me!! LIKED ME! HAHAHAHAHA!!! Rod even told me he still loved me. "FUCK YOU!" was my response, and the fork I'd been carrying, stayed quivering, where I had buried its tines in the bedroom wall.

This period in the story has become a bit blurred with time; long years past and such a muddle of blood and tears, of hurt and loss, of displacement, of substitution and desperation. But no matter how many beers I drank, or cocks I sucked, how many bars and parties I went to or cocks I had in me, the ragged tearing hole left by his presence, his funny snaggle tooth and laughter when he was drunk, his hairy belly, his perfect dick, his attentive lovemaking where I felt we were the only two living souls there were, his generosity of spirit, his kindness, was always there, gaping wide, and my guts spilling. All of those things, so familiar, so expected – pulled away from me and all because I had taken Kenny back to the flat. Ahh, but maybe not. History tells me, and ex-lovers at his funeral told me, that it was going to happen – it happened to them, the pattern was the same, history repeating. What if I hadn't? Well, I don't need to ask do I? If it hadn't been Kenny, it would surely have been someone else, next week, next month, the next bar, the next party – too much cock, too much temptation for a man like him. The grass was always greener. Sadly he failed to water the grass on this side of the fence and it became yellow, then brown then withered away. Rod was NOT a bad man; he was a wonderful loving spirit whom everyone he ever came into contact with adored and wanted to be his friend, confidante, and lover. But he was also a serial philanderer, and being 'cheeky' wasn't enough.

When what was going on became public knowledge, 3 things happened.

1. Kath gave Rod the biggest bollocking he'd ever had in his life, and a massive slap. (Thanks Kath.)

2. Rod and Kenny stopped going to the club (to make it easier for me, apparently! How was that EASIER, exactly? You were just snoggin' him in a DIFFERENT club. You'd still be in my bed when I got back, or come in, all giggly and pissed when I was already home, in bed. HOW, exactly was that easier? NOTHING, EVER, would make it easier, you arse. Easier on your conscience, more like).

And

3. I met someone else.

No1 – Excellent.

No2. – Agony.

No3. – Some light relief from the endless grey, and beer soaked, one night

stands.

ONE.

Richard was his name. A real nice man. Rod, on one of his nights off, asked me out for a drink – there was a new pub open in Stratford. Having little better to do, and leaping like a sad whore at the chance of spending some time with him, I agreed and off we went. It was shit. New, and shit. All horrid neon and poncey décor, with the atmosphere of an abandoned asylum. Anyway, we'd made the effort to go, and maybe after a few drinks, Rod would see sense, see that that Kenny was no good for him and that he wanted me all the time (this did not happen, dear reader, as you may have guessed. That did not happen, in fact, until I was with someone else....), so we kind of hung around, avoiding the drafts and staring around disconsolately, when.....a group, noisy, young, possibly interesting folk tumbled in through the door. One of whom was Richard, who had taught with me, back in the Traveller's days when I took the few travellers that were there at any one time to make it worth the bother into the 'main school'. He was there....that's MY gaydar fucked then! How did I not notice him? Too busy stopping little snots nicking stuff and causing mayhem in the class to notice much else really. Anyway, it seemed to be an after school do......in a gay bar? Maybe Rod'd got it wrong? Actually, he had, the twat. The pub was over the road. No wonder there didn't seem to be many homosexualists hanging around! Pahahahaaa. It was full of 'types', if you know what I mean. The pub was making a valiant attempt at 80s chic and failing miserably. I don't think it stayed open long, not surprisingly. Anyway. I clocked, floppy haired Richard, he clocked me and we both went on with our separate activities: he laughing uproariously with his colleagues, and I being glum and sad and wishing I was dead.

"I don't like it in here, Nige," said Rod. "It's full of dry lunch cunts. Shall we go somewhere else?"

"Um, yeah. OK." ('To bed' was whispering around in my head). "Where?"

"I saw another pub just down the road. Let's try that one, now we're out. May as well, eh?"

As we passed Richard's group, he looked up, smiled and turned back to his (half) pint. We went out in to the Stratford night.

"What about the Pigeons? Oh bollocks. It don't open till 10. Look, over there..." and we crossed the road and went into....the gay pub! Ta DAH!

• • •

"Fuck ME!" Said Rod. *"I knew it was round here somewhere! What do you want, babe? Pint?"*

"Yes. Thankyou." STOP BEING SO FUCKING NORMAL. AND NICE. AND STOP CALLING ME 'BABE'.

It was pretty busy, and Rod was at the bar for ages. I was just standing looking round, when the door swung open and in walked.......no prizes for guessing....Richard.

"I thought I'd find you in here. You went to the wrong pub..."

"Well, yes, we did."

"Is that your boyfriend?" he asked as he spotted Rod coming over with the drinks.

"Erm.....no. no it isn't. Not anymore." (OUCHY HURT HURT). *"We split up, but we still live together."*

"Ah, well, that's good."

What was? That we'd split up? Or that we were two civilised, grown-ups who could behave sensibly in a difficult situation? (HA! If only he knew...)

"Hello, babe," said Rod. *"I'm Rod."* (STOP CALLING PEOPLE BABE!! Unless it's me. No, don't call me babe either, actually.)

"Richard."

"You know each other?"

"A bit. We used to teach together."

"Gawd, fuck me! Not another one! I had enough to put up with from THIS one, when we was together, didn't I Nige?" Guffaw.

What are you doing? I didn't understand all this subtext. I know what you're doing, RODNEY CARR, why don't you just FUCK OFF and leave me with my friend, someone you don't know, that you haven't shagged and someone that, actually, I quite fancy. AND I don't need your permission.

"Richard. Rich", I said, proprietorially, *"Do you want a bevvy?"*

"Aw, you should've said. I'll get it."

"NO, it's FINE, thank you. I will. Rich?"

"Half of lager, please. Any sort."

"Sure. Won't be a minute."

Actually, looking at the crush at the bar, I'd probably be five and Rod'd be there with Richard...unattended.

"Oh actually, Rod", I said, *"We were just going. Weren't we. Rich. Richard. WEREN'T WE?"*

"Oh. Um...yes", he replied, looking a bit confused. *"But I will have that drink first. No worries. I'll go!"* and he disappeared into the crowd. I turned to Rod.

"What are you doing?"

"Who?"

"You."

"Nothing. Why?"

"Yes you were. 'BABE'...you don't even know him."

"Oh, fer fucks sake. How long have you known me? I call EVERYONE babe."

"Well......you were looking at him."

"And......"

"In THAT way."

"I was not!"

"Yes. You were!"

"Oh fer fuck's sake. Grow up. I've had enough of this. This was supposed to be a nice friendly drink, and you're just being a prat."

How could it EVER just be a 'nice friendly drink', you stupid man. My heart hurts, I can't get twinky boy out of my mind, everything you do or says belongs to ME, and my vision of my life, so snatched away...how could it EVER be just that? You are SUCH a fool. And I love you so much I can barely breathe. And I don't want to be here. And I don't want this pint. And I don't want to 'have fun'. I want.... I want....but my thoughts were interrupted by Richard's return.

* * *

"I've given up. Can't get to the bar. Shall we go?" and he looked straight at me. Not Rod. Me.

"Yes," I said. *"Let's."*

And off went we! Not looking back! HA HA HA HAAAAA.

The last time I saw Richard was Stratford, 1982, all romantics meet the same fate someday....actually, this bit of plagiarism is a lie – we met again years later. Different time, different place....

Any hoo.....off we went back to his lickle love nest in the sky, a flat in a nearby tower block. I was pretty pissed by now (no change there then) and I was a smoker of St. Moritz (sad, eh?) and the only really clear memory of that night was burning his coffee table with a fag. We DID have sex; I remember, vaguely, a size issue and a failure of that particular attempt, but we did both reach a satisfactory conclusion. It must've been okay enough to agree to meet up again, and thus began a really decent, healing affair. Nothing desperate, nothing long term, and I believe on his part too (unless he could see that, really, he and we didn't stand a chance) but for quite a few weeks we met up – he'd pick me up in his 2CV (yes. Really) and we'd drive around London and for the first time in some time, I felt peaceful....not ripped, not screaming in silent fury at God/Buddha/Allah/whoever about how unfair and totally shit my life is, and not, in that moment, in that little car, or in Richard's gentle arms, wishing I was elsewhere.

He was a decent man, a considerate lover and he could, I'm sure see the depth of my hurt and did his best to mend it. And, sadly, in the end, failed. He simply couldn't compete. We made love, we had beer, we laughed but all too briefly the dam got washed away and I was once more swept away in the flood of both not being able to be with Rod, at the same time not wanting to be with him cos he was a *CUNT* and gasping for air in all the mixed swirling waters in between. Rich and I just saw each other less, then less and less; I kept making excuses for not meeting and I think a mate of his put him straight, who, being outside could see the blade of doom swinging overhead, like in *'The Pit and the Pendulum'*, coming ever lower to slice us apart. We parted amicably, if a little sadly, both thinking 'in another time, another place', but *mea culpa*. We didn't stand a chance. I didn't ALLOW it to be. He went back to his City Farm and school, and I continued to play charades at PPL in my lickle purple number.

How had I gone from Mr. Lucky, to Mr. Miserable Bastard in such a short time? I had few friends during this time, as all I did was moan about stuff. People were bored but I was so far up my own miserable arse to notice and so of course it was all THEIR fault. Why can't you see I'm sad? That I need a hug? That I need you to be nice to me and LISTEN? The fact that that the few remaining 'mates' had had their fill of listening passed me by. Apart from Chris. Dear old Chris, who like a big ole rescuing type thing erm.....rescued me. He'd seen me plummeting down, waited patiently until it was clear I wasn't going do anything but get pissed and moan a lot, then rang me and said: *"Right. Get dressed. Tube, 8 o clock. If you're not there, I'll come and get you and drag you out by your big girly hair."*

Remembering previous nights out with Chris, I wasn't desperately keen. Here are a couple of examples:

He decided one time, it would be good to go to 'Heaven', under the Arches at Charing Cross. I unwillingly agreed, but went. After paying a HUGE amount of money to get in (about eight quid, I think, but this did entitle you to go through to the Eagle, a side bar where you get could get tied up and fucked for free; there's another tale to tell here, folks. Not for *your* ears, gentle reader.) We went in and, Lordy Lordy....men. Thousands of men. Mostly stripped to the waist, mostly dancing to that there 'Hi-NRG' nonsense.... (you can take the boy out of Cornwall....) but many snoggin', staring, drinking.....it was like...like... I don't know what it was like, to be honest. Anyway, we stood around like twats, well, I did. Chris had disappeared. Boom. Just like that. Cheers matey. So I stood. Got another beer, with a 2nd mortgage, and stood around some more. Chris reappeared, slightly sweaty and a bit goggle eyed (I didn't ask, and don't know to this day) and said:

"You dancing'?"

"You askin'?" (Bad Scouse accent).

"No, not really. Mine's a lager. Back in a minute!" and he disappeared into the crowd again.

I went to the bar. I wandered about a bit, trying not to stare. I looked into the Eagle (OH MY GOODNESS!!!), and went back to the original spot, waiting for my 'friend'. Who never reappeared. So I drank his drink too, gave it another ten minutes and said to the bloke who was eyeing me up (I was a looker in them days you know. Amongst all those buff, cropped shirtless men, I was 'interesting' with me bouffant mullet and bri-nylon), *"I'm off. If my mate arrives tell him I've fucked off home. Oh. And that he's a bastard. Cheers."*

And I left. Lovely. Thanks for that.

Another time he decided it would be a good idea to try to blag our way into Napoleons, in Bond Street, a members only club for 'the older gentleman' with LOADSA MAHNEY......quite HOW we would manage this was never made clear, but off we went, me in tow, on our latest ridiculous adventure which was bound to end in disaster.

So, there it was, all lit, subtle – like, with a few lads (that I now know, of course, to be rent boys) and Mercs and Bentleys pulling up outside.

"You ARE joking, aren't you?"

No, come on. It'll be fun."

"Exactly HOW will it be fun? And, what happens if we DO get inside?"

"Stop fuckin moanin', and enjoy yourself for once. If we get in, they'll buy us drinks. You can get a shag if you want. Mine's a lager if anyone asks."

So, we stood around outside the club, with the milling hordes of whores and young men looking for love, sex, alcohol or money, or any combination of those. It was both fascinating and sad, worrying and thrilling. After a while this man, really old, about 45, came over and said: *"DO you want to come in?"* ME!! Out of all those young twinks.

"Not unless my mate comes too," I said firmly. So he gestured to Chris, who was looking both annoyed and hopeful and took us both inside, waving at the doorman as we passed.

"FUCK. ING. HELL!!" said Chris, staring round. This was opulence indeed. Mr. Bloke asked what we'd like to drink – *"Have anything you like, boys! Anything!"*

I was rather thinking of a fabulous cocktail with a sparkler or something but...

"I'll have a lager," said Chris.

"Oh. Me too then."

I supposed he was up for a threesome with a couple of rough types – we weren't exactly dressed up *marché* – but he was shit out of luck (as my sainted Lady Mother used to say) if he thought I was going to shag Chris. Ewwwww! He was my SISTER!! Maybe he wanted to watch? Make a video? This was getting weirder by the minute.

He came back with the drinks. *"Hi,"* he drawled. *"I'm Rupert."* (It probably wasn't, but this WAS 30 odd years ago!)

"Hello!" I said. *"I'm Mike and this is erm...Mark."* (False names. Seemed safer.) *"Thank you for the drinks."*

"A pleasure, to be sure. I have some friends I'd like you to meet. They like boys your age, your type. A bit rough, a bit thick looking."

Excuse me? Thick looking? Fucking cheek! I have a Cert. Ed, you know. What? Was I being purloined here, for sex by a gang of old blokes? Maybe I'd be whisked off and sold into sex slavery? Actually, that one with the salt n pepper hair isn't too....WHOA! Hang on.....

Erm, maybe a bit later? Mark and me, well, we're a bit shy...."

"OK, then er...MIKE." (He knew HE KNEW!!) *"Come over when you're ready.....don't leave it too long though; there are lots of others who would jump at the chance. Come over when you feel like a little Veuve Clicquot....."*

Ooooh, I like champagne, me I do. *"Pssst Chris......"* whispering, far too loudly...."*CHRIS...... Shall we go over? Look, they got champagne!"*

"No, you fucking idiot. They'll think you're rent and you'd have to 'cough up' so to speak, in return."

"Just because you don't like older men (WOW!! That's the first time I'd articulated my 'preference'.) *doesn't mean we shouldn't go over. We can always just say NO."*

"How can you be so fuckin NAÏVE? How old are YOU? Twelve? You can't say NO. That's the point. YOU drink their champagne, they get to fuck you. That's the rules. All of 'em probably. At the same time."

Chris has always been my torment and my saviour. I hated him and I loved him and once again he was right, but I had my beer goggles on and it DID seem like an attractive proposition – well, THAT one did and maybe the others wouldn't mind if their friend and me had an affair and eventually got a house together and everything?

"I'll just have one glass."

"No. No, you fucking WON'T. Stay here with me."

Something in his tone brought me out of my (ridiculous) fantasy and back to the present.

"Look," he said, *"Let's just have another drink. I need a wazz. Mine's a lager."*

So I went up to the bar and ordered two pints.

"That's three hundred pounds please," said the barman. It wasn't obviously, but it might as well have been.

"But I've only got a fiver..."

"Well then maybe you shouldn't be in here," he said. *"Who are you with? Where is your admitting member?"*

"Um..... he's...he's......" But Mr. Rupert was nowhere to be seen. *"Um...I don't know actually."*

"Well, then you need to leave."

"Yes, but, my friend is......."

"NOW."

As if summoned by some supernatural force or a wave of a wand that conjured up fucking HUGE blokes, two bouncers appeared and picked me up, literally, feet –off – the – floor stylee, and levitated me out of the door and dumped me on the pavement. I HAD JUST BEEN THROWN OUT OF NAPOLEON'S! How fucking cool is that? Moments later, Chris appeared, shouting *"You can stick your poncey club up yer fuckin arse!!"*....and there was Roops. With two other young fellow – me – lads. As they walked past, he said, *"You should've had the champagne when you had the chance. Now fuck off, you losers."*

"NO, YOU FUCK OFF, YOU SLIMY OLD CUNT!" bellowed Chris. *"That was good, eh? Come on! Where shall we go now?"*

"Home, please. Just home."

"Lightweight."

But he took me home. A saviour.

As I said, nights out with Chris were nothing if not 'interesting'.

So, back to this night...

● ● ●

I DID get dressed, mostly because I KNEW he WOULD come round and drag me out by my girly hair, and met him at the Tube, at 8.00.

"We're going somewhere new now. It's called 'The London Apprentice'. You'll like it."

I wasn't sure I would but, I didn't have much choice. He was on a mission, a mission to save his best friend. And get a few beers for free, of course. I don't think in all the years I knew him, he'd EVER got a round in. Respect. I loved him, the old bastard. What he HADN'T told me was that this was a leather bar, or at least, full of proper hard blokes, in their lumberjack shirts, torn jeans and a rainbow of coloured hankies in their back pockets. Once again, I looked like a prize twat.

"Not as good as the Colherne, but nearer," he said.

"Is yours a lager?"

"HAHAHAHAAAA. Fuck off." he said as he disappeared to the bogs.

Actually it was quite nice. Nice beer, nice 'eye candy' (See? I was learning!), nice music, if you liked Divine and Evelyn Thomas....perhaps he was right. This WAS what I needed, instead of moping around at home. We had more beer, the scenery improved. People seemed friendly enough. Very friendly, actually, as Chris was at the bar with his tongue down the throat of some skinhead type. So. That's me then. Twatty gooseberry or whatever the expression is for someone who is always left alone in clubs when their best friend and person who brought them cops off with someone. Again. Wallflower. Yeah, that's it.

The L.A., Old Street, long since closed.

TWO.

"You look a bit fed up," said someone, in my ear, above Hazell Dean moaning that she was 'searchin, and lookin' for love', at 130 beats per minute. *"You been deserted?"*

"Erm, not exactly. My friend," – I nodded to Chris, who was having the top of his head licked – *"brought me, and now he's....otherwise engaged. It's alright. It happens all the time."*

"Ah. So I see. That's a bit weird, eh? Licking someone's head?"

"You haven't seen anything," I replied. *"That's nothing...."* And we laughed. Together.

We were standing at one of those funny little shelf things attached to pillars, and I had my elbows on it and the next thing, I felt something in my palm; a finger circling, gently, circling, circling.

"Hi. I'm Ken," said the man and I looked at him then and my heart kind of juddered. He looked to be the kindest man, with the gentlest and bluest eyes I had ever seen. *"Hello,"* I said.

We chatted a while and I realised he was South African – he had a marvellous burr to his voice; musical, lilting.

"Shall we go somewhere quieter?" he said. *"Like, Jim's Phone Bar. Bit camp, but at least we can hear each other."*

"Yes, sure OK. Let me just tell...."

"He wouldn't be interested, I don't think."

I turned to look where Chris had been standing, by the bar and all I could see now was his new squeeze gazing at the ceiling and just the top of Chris's head as it went backwards and forwards.

"You're probably right. Let's go." And he took me by the hand and he took me by the heart and we left the L.A., and I struck out into waters new.

We went to the phone bar – a cute little place with phones on the tables so you could ring someone up, across the room and.....I don't know. Say: "You *want a drink?*" "*My friend fancies you*". Wanna shag? Talk about the meaning of Life"? What a weird concept – why don't you just go ACROSS the room and ask? Anyway, I wouldn't like the risk that everyone'd be on the phone. Except me. It was quiet; (well – that's a relative term, and at least I didn't have to watch my best mate giving someone he'd only just met a blow job. These were still my days of innocence, dear reader. I was only about 4, in gay years), we found a table, and I went to the bar.

"Beer? A short?"

"No. Orange juice. Thank you." (What a polite young man!)

"You're not driving, are you?"

"No, I'm a recovering alcoholic." BLAM. Just like that. I wasn't quite sure how to follow that up.

"Oh. Um. Right. Maybe I'll have juice too."

"No, silly. You go ahead. I'm used to it."

{It will help you enormously to get into the spirit of things if you read any conversations between us in an Afrikaans accent. His bits, I mean.)

We sat and we talked. Just that. And we smiled. REALLY smiled, with pleasure, with amusement. And we laughed. Man, what a strange sensation in my face! All my smiling muscles seemed to have atrophied, and it felt strange, but wonderful, to be back in the real world, where most folks smiled and laughed all the time. And we talked some more and had an evening of joyous uncomplicated pleasure, the coming together of two brand new people, sharing those first intimacies, those first secrets.

We finished our drinks – it seemed a little insensitive to have another – and we stood up, in to that thousand year silence. Now what? Shake hands, and say, *"Well, it was lovely to meet you"*? A peck on the cheek, before going our separate ways? No. Here's what happened. Ken took my hand and again drew little circles on my palm, something secret and quiet he would do all through our time together, which would I'm sure have been long and happy if I hadn't been such an utter fucking twat. However....he drew gently on my palm, like some arcane mating symbol and with that it, was decided. We would be together this night, and many after that.

We made the decision to go back to Cranbrook Road. Mostly because Ken had someone called Nicky living in his flat and she was seeing her (married) boyfriend this evening – he was a fireman (and seriously sexy) and they didn't get much 'fokking time' so it would be good to go somewhere else. I was unsure of Rod's whereabouts. It was a Friday night and he was probably down the club, licking his wounds, left by Kenny who didn't love him QUITE that much after all.....he'd stopped coming round to the flat, and they didn't meet up much anymore. I still don't know who did what to whom. Or who DIDN'T do what to who, or who did what to somebody else....anyway, they'd 'split up', from whatever the relationship was; something flimsy, something made of air. Rod had disappeared down to Brighton for a few days, to be nursed and Bovrilled by his Auntie Jan, and when he came back he was all tail between leggy and way too nice. TOO. FUCKING. LATE. MATE.

Anyway that night, Ken and I went back to Ilford and there began a time of sweet surrender, of gentleness and loving arms. He was a genuine and honest man, whose penis was unfortunately too large for most things (we managed to find alternatives) and who's troubled past put mine well and truly into perspective.

He was in this flat, in fact in this LIFE, because he had been too drunk to even commit suicide. The black cab he had tried to throw himself in front of was actually further away and going slower than he had thought and he ended up just throwing himself onto the road, and cracking his head. In A+E they told him that he didn't need a taxi – booze would kill him soon enough, but more slowly and infinitely more unpleasantly. From that moment he admitted he was a drunk, enrolled on the 12 Steps, got a flat and sorted himself out. All this he told me that night in the Phone bar, (or some of it – most of that glowing evening we spent laughing and gently, unwittingly falling into each other's hearts. Not too much nasty stuff please, not yet, not now) but it all came out as he gave me his trust and his heart and his soul. Ah, poor Ken. Such a mistake for you. And I am truly, truly sorry.

He had, back home, been a committed Jehovah's Witness, with a wife and two beautiful children - a photograph, creased, repeatedly viewed - blonde, like him, smiling across continents at a father whose heart would never heal. He had done all the things that he had been taught and told, behaved properly and lovingly to his family, to the fellowship and to God. Unfortunately he also he loved cock. What torment of conscience and soul searching he must have endured, knowing the punishment he would suffer in the fires of hell. And it seems, his faith kept him on the path. He delivered The Watchtower, went to the Kingdom Hall for lessons, loved his wife and children and was generally loved by God for his good works. But, he loved cock too. And, while there was nothing, NOTHING, to be done about that fact, his love of his life and his faith kept him from the pit. Until, until, one day, on a Sunday, on a family outing with his best friend and their families, Ken was spotted, on the lake, sucking his best friend's cock, by another Witness, who was in another boat. Blissfully unaware on the shore, the wives chattered and the children all played, unaware of the catastrophe that was about to befall them.

Ken didn't KNOW he'd been seen, and carried on as normal, until he was summoned by a congregation of elders. He must have known, then, somehow, that he was doomed. He was *Disfellowshipped*, the 'expelling and subsequent shunning of such an unrepentant wrongdoer'. It is the strongest form of discipline, administered to an offender deemed unrepentant. He wasn't unrepentant but in truth there was nothing he could do. Promising never to do it again would have been pointless. He was too emotionally intelligent to know that for the lie it would be and that it would only be a matter of time, a matter of opportunity before anther erection presented itself and he would fall once more, into that pit, into those fires of Hell. I cannot imagine what this must have been like for him – for *anyone*, let alone for this sorrowful, gentlest of men, the one sat weeping before me, and it must have been the end of the world. It was the end of HIS world, that's for sure. He was considered to be past 'shepherding', and received no visits, no counselling, no help, no support or love from the Elders, the church or his friends. His wife then disowned him, forbade him contact with his children and effectively he was alone and cut adrift in a world he barely understood, filled with longings that brought him pain and shame. Coming out is fucking hard enough, but with the weight of Satan and eternal damnation to deal with too....it's no surprise he sought to numb the pain and turned to alcohol. He left the land of his birth, shunned and alone and came to London where he somehow, in the way only a dedicated drunk can, proceeded to hold down a job, get a flat – the one we were sat in, as I listened in horror to this tale – and got paralytically drunk in the way only an alcoholic can. Every day, and every night he drank, until the time came when the pain of his missing wife and girls became too much and he stepped out, in Oxford Street, in to the path of a black cab which due to his drunken eyes was further away than he thought, to make it stop. Just to make it stop. And in a way, it did. Here he was. Brave, handsome and sober, and about to fall so deeply in love with me – like the 'Steve' moment had been for me, a vindication that maybe, somehow, all the pain had been worth it – that he would never recover. I was now his drug; I kept him upright. My guilt is absolute.

It is not my job to criticise anybody's religion or belief system, but where, WHERE was the humanity in the way Ken was treated by his so-called Christian brethren? Where was the compassion, the empathy, the support for him? Yes, he was different. Yes, he did not conform to your ideals, but surely Christ taught love for all people? It was you, you and your intransigent Jehovah, that threw him in front of that cab, and for that I say, thirty years on, shame, SHAME on you.

Oooh. I don't normally rant like that! But I have clear memories of the evening Ken opened his heart, and his wounds, to me – the loss of his wife, his children, his country, his Nationhood, all unbearable to him. Until he met me. I, according to letters I STILL have, and I quote (Ken, if you ever read this, forgive me; it is a part of our narrative and it is nothing but true)

"Our ability to communicate and the realisation that you actually offered to perceive and understand my wretchedness was as big a bonus as our mutual love. Hence, the inconsiderate and gathering momentum of my need for you...."

Ken was nothing if emotionally articulate and we deepened our passion at a giddy rate. Lionel Ritchie was the soundtrack of our love, '*All Night Long....*'

'Karamu, fiesta, forever'...that's what it felt like. All flicker and full of light. We went to the Indian and roared with laughter when he said he *would "try the gulab, but could he have them without jam on"*... (true!!). We, or rather, I, drank beer for pleasure not need or loneliness and he said he didn't mind; he went to his meetings and returned, refreshed and powerful; we went to Selina's, My BOYFRIEND and me, and we rubbed our crotches together to Irene Cara and *"What a Feeling!"* and suddenly found ourselves alone on the dance floor, bumping and grinding while the watching crowd whooped and cheered (until we had to stop because, as I mentioned, Ken was rather large in the penis department and he became 'embarrassed' , if you get my drift); we went to Brighton for the weekend with his friends and got a hotel and we only went out once, the rest of the time was spent fucking in our room; we sat on the shingle shore revelling in our luck while the waves crashed and ssshhhhh-ed in front of us; we drove home in silence with his hand down the back of my jeans and his fingers up my bum, giggling with our secret and hard and impatient for the journey to end; we laughed and farted (initially, much to his horror and ESPECIALLY at that particular moment) and we healed each other, stitched back up the wounds our respective pasts had inflicted upon us, in our wars and lives, and found solace and peace in each other's arms and silence.

I was still living – or rather, *rooming* – at Cranbrook road, and saw Rod less and less. He seemed to like Ken, or at least, made no play for him, or tried to spoil things. We split the time between there and the majestically named John

Drinkwater Tower, where Ken's flat was. The Eleventh Floor balcony was where I stood and heard the news of Torville and Dean getting nine perfect sixes in Sarajevo, watching people celebrating at the bus stop down below, as they read their Evening Standards. The eleventh floor and the lift actually worked – although it was never quite the same after I farted in it, almost melting the aluminium and stripping the posters from the walls. It was a Monday morning and I had had a sleepover after a few beers and a curry and was all in cerise and on my way to work. The doors opened. I got in. I farted, and I mean FARTED. A miasma of green fumes filled the lift and then on floor five the doors opened and an Asian family got in. I died a death. I'm not sure if I was relieved that they walked in, turned round and made a dash for the doors before they closed, trapping them in this box of foul fumes. I didn't know quite what to do…..I just got to the ground floor, and scuttled off to the bus stop.

Anyway, I digress …..I was still worked for PPL, still putting up with all the tit and cunt jokes all day, but hey, it paid the bills and it was reasonable money. The end came quite suddenly though when it did. I was due to be Runner for the day. But when I woke that morning, I had a really really bad back. I don't know why – Ken hadn't been there the night before so it wasn't THAT; it just hurt. I rang in and tried to throw a sickie. Unfortunately, and typically, they were short staffed and persuaded me to go in on the condition that I could change vans, and be the Back Man. As that meant sitting on me arse all day, and not losing any pay, I agreed, got dressed and struggled in, in a martyrly sort of way.

"Oy, Bray. You're in van fackin 651. 'Urry up, you cahnt, you're already late".

Charming. I could barely walk but got up in to the van and off we went. I don't remember the run, but we were over the river when a call came in over the radio that there had been an 'incident' at Belsize Park and that all vehicles were to return to base immediately. We turned round and headed back to Ilford, alarmed and at great speed.

We were all assembled in the Mosh Pit, as I now called it, and the Guv'nor came in with the news that the Runner, on the North London run, whilst carrying the cash bags back to the van, at Belsize Park Tube, had been shot dead. It seems that, despite the rule we all knew – LET THE FUCKING BAG GO!!!! – the strap had caught on his wrist and he hadn't been able to – and the kid shot him. Gone. Just like that.

Apart from the shock of this, of losing a colleague, who was in fact one of the nicer ones, a bit higher up the food chain than the others here, there came an even bigger realisation - I hope you're keeping up, you lot. Yep. MY run that day. MY job that day. Fuck. FUCKFUCKFUCKFUCK. That would have been me. Maybe the bag wouldn't have snagged, who knows, but there would still have been a crazy little fuckwit with a gun.

I left the next day. Don't say *"Oooh, it was only a one off. It wouldn't happen again"*. You don't know that, and I certainly wasn't going to risk it. We were all dismissed; all the vans locked down and we all went home. Sitting in the bus, with my back pain worse, I thanked every conceivable god for sciatica and never went back. I left my darling purple garb on their doorstep and went down the pub on Ilford High Street. Karma Chameleon was on the Jukebox.

Mr. Lucky. Mr. V. Bloody Lucky.

I have often wondered what the outcome of that was and have discovered in the course of writing this that the 'young man' was tried by no other than Richard Ferguson QC, who went on to defend the Brighton Bombers and Rosemary West (which was unusual in that it was the first case to be tried in defence of the accused who was already dead!). The boy was found guilty of manslaughter....he 'didn't mean to kill' my friend, apparently. You still did though. And you might have killed me.

'In May 1984, within weeks of his arrival in England, the Ulster barrister Richard Ferguson, who has died aged 73, received his first brief, when he was invited to defend a young man accused of the murder of a security guard killed at point-blank range in a robbery at Belsize Park tube station in north London.' This is from his obituary, in the Guardian, dated August 11th, 2009, when he died. I wonder if HE remembered that boy, from 25 years before. The family shattered that day? I do.

So I was unemployed again (but alive, and no longer having to answer being asked if I thought *'she'd let me fuck her if I showed her my cock'*, and making comments on the size of her tits and taking bets on whether she *'shaved her fanny or not'*. There were advantages in all things) and, whatever, there were still bills to pay. I realised the best way to minimize my outgoings was to move out! Easy peasy!

So, that's what I did. I moved over to Leytonstone in to Ken's flat. He of course was overjoyed. Poor Nicky was not – it was her little love nest where she could have her illicit tryst in peace (Ken was nothing if not obliging. I guess having been so harshly judged himself, he rather erred on the side of generosity). It was OK for a while, but we were sleeping on a crappy sofa bed in the lounge,

• • •
88

while they had his big proper bed for shagging a couple of times a week. Eventually, he asked to swap (much to my relief) and not long after that Nicky moved out – I don't know where she went but it was amicable I think. Anyway, that left us to pursue our carnal interests more freely. We discovered, eventually, after much perseverance, (and it turned out, alcoholism has nothing to do with Amyl Nitrate) a way to fit a quart into a pint pot and thereafter we were happy as sand boys.

Christmas '83 and at last – Mr. Lucky was happy and safe. My sister came up to stay, and she brought Sam, her daughter (Get her used to the gay boys early! Nice one!) and we had the best of times. The North Star, disastrously close to the Tower was where we went, Gill and I, 'just for a quick pint before dinner', got completely legless and were still in the pub, full of Christmas cheer/beer and Ken arrived about two hours later, with a 'where the fucking hell have you been' kinda glower. We persuaded him to have one for the M11, then two and finally realised that we really SHOULD stop now and *"OOOH! Fuck where's' me daughter?"* Ken had locked her in the flat to come and fetch us, but that didn't go exactly according to plan. By the time we fell in through the door, full of giggle shame, Sam was pissed. She had found a bottle of vodka under the sink (Nicky's?) and had drunk half of it. We found her throwing up in the bathroom. Please do not ring Social Services. We, or actually Ken, put her to bed, where she threw up some more little haystacks on the duvet. Gill and I meanwhile tried to get in the cupboard under the sink, for a laugh.

Later, we decided to go down the club – I have no recollection of any food; I am hoping, in a retrospectively guilty kind of way that Ken had not actually got round to doing it. Sam washed her hair, and still drunk, tried to dry it with a hair dryer she'd found.

"Can anyone smell burning?" said Gill.

"MUUUUUUM!" yelled Sam and there she was, smoke coming off her head where she had put the hair dryer directly onto her scalp.

"My hair's on fire."

We rushed her back to the bathroom and dunked her under the tap.

Later, after a bit of a nap, in the process of getting ready, Ken decided he needed to bath before we went out, and was doing just that when Sam decided she 'needed a poo. Right now!' So we had to let her into the bathroom, where Ken sat in the bath, vainly trying to hide his genitals from this small, female child with a flannel that didn't fit, for reasons I have already explained. She didn't, fortunately, have a poo right then as it wasn't really 'convenient'. Ken cut short his bath time and went to get dressed. Gill and I were sitting in lounge, waiting for Sam to finish her hair and in walked Ken in the underpants that Gill had bought him for Christmas. Modestly had forbidden me to explain fully to her his erm...endowment to her, with the result that there he stood, in his new red pants, with the end of his knob poking up over the waistband, and one bollock hanging out of the leg. My, how we laughed.

"They're a but tyny, but thenks!" he said, and disappeared, fortunately not meeting Sam in the corridor.

We did go to Selina's that night, but I really have nothing to tell you; my only memory is of my niece, sitting on a bar stool, in a throbbing gay bar, surrounded by a mass of whooping homos, with a stack of party hats on yelling, above the din: *"GOT ANY WHAAAAAM! AVE EE?"* in a broad Cornish accent. Happy Christmas everyone!

I look back, marvelling at Ken's patience that day, and many days more, when I behaved abominably and he just allowed it, the inconvenience or embarrassment or annoyance always outweighed by the joy he had found in my company and the deep abiding love he had for me.

Islands in the stream

That is what we are

sang Kenny and Dolly, in the chart that week. And we were, buffeted by the waters that had somehow brought us together, full of astonishment to have reached dry land, at last.

Me and Ken, in happier times.

The North Star. Sitting in the shadow of the Tower, long since demolished. Far too close, too convenient. Tiny, smoky, meety-uppy; I usually met my darling Ken in there after work, he with his juice if he was there first, and me with me beer if it was me. We would be happy, so happy to see each other - really, like puppies. We would have a drink together, then leave for the flat, have a quick snog in the lift on the way up and then tumble in – to the sofa, to the bed, to the floor, hard, raging, eager – the early days of lust were all consuming – good for me as it got Rod out of my head for that flame-filled time and good for Ken as it was a luxury, a gift, allowed, really properly allowed with no shame, no retribution and no sense of looming disaster. We fucked, we laughed, and we (I) drank. We did the things that lovers do, like Billy Ocean said. But that wasn't the whole picture – storm clouds were gathering.

The North Star, Leytonstone. The Scene of Many Joys and Sorrows.

We continued going to Selina's as we felt comfortable there and it was also a short walk (and stagger back in my case) down the High Road. It was full of people we knew, and who enfolded us. Rod was there occasionally and it was easier, and easier. He'd buy Ken a drink, like there were no hard feelings and we'd have a chat, but NOT, I repeat, NOT reminisce.....any conversation that included the lines: *"Do you remember when we…"* was quickly shut down or glided over. Of course Ken was aware of what had happened and was gentle and understanding, as he was in all things. He loved me, therefore all was well. My references to members of Rod's family were taken as just that – memories, recollections, and my "Bad Rod Days", as he referred to them, seemed to be less frequent.

But, of course, they weren't……my mind was always half with Ken, half with my Jewish Nemesis. I tried I swear, I tried, but as Kylie once said *"Can't get you outa my head".* Disaster loomed and I was unable to stop it. It was a train, coming down the track, its big cowcatcher poised to scoop me up and bear me away to the land of Pain. Well, both of us really. Ken, I did my best. You were the gentlest of men and the most undeserving of what happened.

It was New Year.'83. Rod's brother Tony was having a 'do'. They were always massive – Tony had a few quid and loved to share it – and we had no other plans. Well, actually we did – we were invited to the Club, and another party but no! I said, this one'll be FAB! And it was. For me, at least. All the family was there and I felt at home and loved and cocooned in the heart of these people. And, I had really really missed them. They all treated Ken with kindness and made him welcome in the way that they always did and we partied and partied until I had crossed the Rubicon….I drank, Ken obviously didn't and as the evening wore on, my beer goggles were focusing in only one direction. That fucking baldy bastard over there, the one with the vodka and cokes, the one with the crooked smile, the bit of belly hair showing, the ready open laugh and mis-timed dance moves.

BAP BAP! BADADADADDA BAP BAP went George Benson. And there it was.

The end.

"Come on Nige! I love this one!" yelled my heroin, and he grabbed me and held me up close and did that thing with his hips – a kind of double hitch step; very clever and very sexy – and I was gone. He knew it, I knew and Ken knew it. Nothing was said, we just danced and everyone was singing *"When there's music in the air an' lovin' everywhere, gimme the night!"* their heads back and

their drunken mouths agape, and trying to dance like black guys and failing miserably, and Ken stood over by the bar with Cousin Doreen, who had her hand on his shoulder, comfortingly, like she knew and was trying to rub away the pain, watching. Just watching and trying to prepare himself.

The night wore on drunkenly, and Ken the only sober one in the room, battled on. A room full of people he had never met, all pissed, all one, all united, all one unit, one universe with him orbiting far out, in the cold space of not belonging. Eventually it was over, I was pissed as a fart and was sick on the pavement outside the flats. *"Lucky it wasn't in the lift, eh?"* said Ken as he helped me up to bed.

Ken, Doreen and me, New Year's Eve, 1983

The next day, a brand new year, began with me and the hangover from hell. *"Did you have a good time?"* I asked somewhat naively. *"I don't remember much after about 12. We did 'Auld Lang Syne' didn't we? God, that Tony, he always puts on a party, eh? Did I behave? Well, would've had to, with all the family there, eh?"*

At this point I was back, in the absence of anything else, trying to sell insurance (unsuccessfully) and doing a bit of bar work at the club. The insurance thing took me around the Ilford area – they were warm leads and had to be followed up by, in this case, a completely useless salesman who just went *"Oh, OK, then Bye"* as soon as the customer said *"We got / don't want / fuck off with your insurance."* I still didn't manage to sell a single policy (or earn a single penny – good job for the bar and Ken's decent wage) but what I DID get was the chance to go a-visiting, as my time was my own, so I went to see Kath most afternoons (who had always been an ally over the breakup with her "fuckin stupid cunt" of a brother) and so I could go round there, have a wee gin and slag him off. Then, I could go across the road. And *suck* him off.

NO, wait! Let me try to explain! Justify this monstrous situation! Actually I can't - it was just bad, bad bad and really unfair to everyone.

Rod had had to sell the flat in Cranbrook Road; he probably couldn't afford it after I'd left (TOUGH SHIT I SAY) and he'd got a little one bedroom flat, opposite his sister.

So. Ken is at work and looking forward to coming home to the man he had given his heart and soul to, earning money to keep us both going; Kath is one side of the road sitting with me agreeing with her rant about what a shit her brother was and how he should've kept it in his pants and he was going to end a lonely old man and serves him fuckin well right; Rod is at home, by arrangement, waiting for me to 'pop in' to say Hello. We had sex. Every time. And it was glorious and sweaty and as beautiful, in those moments as it had ever been. On one occasion, I rang Ken to say I was going to be late home – a difficult client, you know – and I was on the phone and Rod is standing on the bed, poking his erection in to my face and rubbing it along the back of my neck, while I tried to keep my breathing rate as normal as I could. I MUST'VE smelled of sex, of sweat when I got home on those occasions, but if I did, he never said. A gallant loser.

So, as I say – how can I explain? How can I justify this behaviour? I can't. It was what it was. I was utterly addicted to this man and there was nothing I could do. I was a junkie, a smack head, an addict and would have let nothing stand in the way of my next fix.

Clearly this was untenable. Ken knew, saw, felt things were different. His attempts to make love were rebuffed – *"Will you get off? I'm trying to watch 'The Thorn Birds.'* I was lying on the floor in front of the telly; he started kissing my neck and then tried to bum me....Cast off in favour of Richard Chamberlain. It went from *'I'm not really in the mood,'* to *'I really don't want to do that,'* and eventually to *'Look, it really hurts and I don't want to, ok?'* Cruel things, hurtful things, but I didn't want Ken's cock now, as beautiful as it was because, though he didn't know it, I had Rod's again. I was often late back, I was earning no money, mostly because I wasn't visiting any clients, and I was at Rod's. Maybe he thought I was having an extended 'Bad Rod' time, brought on by the New Year party, clinging vainly to the wreckage as our ship broke up around us.

Then Rod asked me to move back in.

● ● ●

So I did.

I know, gentle reader, exactly what you're thinking. It is one of these three things:

1. You fucking IDIOT! You've got a man who loves you with his heart and soul and you're DUMPING him???

2. Don't do it! Ee ain't wurf it.

Or

3. Poor Ken. Why didn't he see this coming? Oh, btw, you're a heartless cunt.

Any one, or all three of these are valid.

It ended quickly. There wasn't much else to say. Ken said he knew things were all wrong, that at the party he was drowning, but expected maybe I would throw him a life line. I really didn't know just how sad he was; too wrapped up in my own joy at 'going home', I didn't see the overwhelming grief I had caused.

I received a letter from him, in his strange and original handwriting, that I am looking at now, as I write and I am still, 30 years on, moved to tears, and filled with shame.

"I gave you my soul and you took it. You basked in the warmth of it and healed. To me, you gave the most wonderful sense of security, constancy. I redeveloped a purpose in my love of life. …

…I have salvaged no fond memories or warm sensations from us. All my recollections and moments are a source of pain so overwhelming, I am unable to function. I will endeavour to blot them out. I will no doubt survive. One unfortunate aspect that I now hate my flat as much as I once loved it. It is a memorial to my misery. Better, I suppose that it is the flat and not you that is the object of my detestation.

Forgive me for indulging in this letter. Of everyone, I imagine you perceive most, the length and depth of my grief, having been the recipient of my love. I assure you that after our next awkward but inevitable meeting, I will exert supreme effort to conduct myself in the polite and civilised manner of a grown man.

I wish you well, and I adore you. Ken"

The most crucifying thing is his politeness, his civility amidst the now chaos of his life. I weep for him even now, even knowing as I do, he is well and happy and in a wonderful relationship. I broke his heart, the heart that amidst all his own pain, he gave me. Yet, and here is the MOST shameful thing of all, in the whole sorry episode, I went, and didn't even look back. So focussed was I on the man I loved, truly loved, despite all the shit we'd been through, in spite of all the shitty things he'd done, I just packed my backs and left. Back to Rod's, leaving Ken standing amidst his shattered dreams.

Fortunately, he had a good friend, from work I think, Paul, who I saw him with, that 'next, inevitable meeting'. I went back to E11, and decided to drop in to the North Star, I dunno – for old time's sake, and there they were, in OUR seats, at the end of the bar, both with pints. BOTH with pints. I couldn't pretend not to have seen them and, as he had said, it WAS extremely awkward.

"Hi," said Ken.

"Hi," I said.

"This is Paul."

"Hi Paul."

Silence. No proffered hand.

"Erm.....drink, anyone?"

"No thanks," said Ken, *"We're off soon. Just dropped by to get something from upstairs."*

I wonder to this day whether he may have been hoping to see me there, but I had gone, leaving only traces of my Aramis. However...

"Oh, OK. Um........well, it was nice to...." I didn't quite know how to proceed, but the situation was resolved when Paul stood up and threw his pint in my face. *"Why don't you just FUCK OFF, you heartless bastard?"* Sotto voce, so no one would know what was happening, other than I was completely soaked with his pint of Murphys.

They brushed by me, through the silent pub, and as Ken passed, he even had the grace to apologise.

"Look, sorry mate. He's just angry..... Sorry about your shirt. And everything." Standing there, dripping in beer, I just wanted to hold him, smooth him, rub away the scars I had left, but they just kept walking and it was some months before I saw him again, strangely enough, back in the L.A., where it had all

begun, a Universe away. I often wonder, as you do, how my life would have turned out if I had been stronger / braver / less stupid / kinder / less blinkered / more growed up. Ken was a lovely man and I was happy that Paul was there. It quickly turned to love, by all accounts, and he found peace again and I felt less of a cunt. Result all round.

So, I was back in the bed where I belonged. It was all very honeymooney, and extremely cramped. But we were together again, all loved up and that was all that mattered. Wasn't it? Wasn't it? Well actually no it wasn't.

After a week Rod decided it wasn't working and said it was probably better that I moved out! Hurrah! A perfect end.

So there I was, back in the flat, with Nicky, who had had a similar meltdown, but like Ken, I now hated the flat. It smelled of death and sorrow and so I thought I'd look around, ask around for somewhere else. Rod, Richard, Ken, Rod....now what? I didn't really know anything else, and here I was – 28 and YFS. Didn't like it much – I know! I'll get another BF!! Honestly, Bray – you haven't got the sense you were born with.

I began going back to the Club on a regular basis – I got more bar work and a room share in a house opposite Wanstead Park with Tony and two lesbians. One of them was a club singer and 'Bruna and the Boys' used to gig at the club quite often. Tony, a lovely little gay boy, all bouffant and hairsprayed, mentioned there was a room at his place, going so I accepted. And so began another chapter – back on the bevvy, staying up too late, having too much sex (Big chops cos I was the barman, and therefore v. desirable. Not sure how that worked but anyway – who cared? Upped my shag rate no end!). Me and Tony became really close, even sharing clothes - he was much younger than me and I probably looked a twat, but I was sore, hurting and anything that cheered me up was welcome.

The Flats, across which I had to walk, as well as being the location of the aforementioned Dames Road Cottage, was a pretty busy cruising spot – a bit like Hampstead Heath but not so posh and with less trees. Several times I had a quickie on the way home from work – once I got followed by a very nice cub on a bike; we had a quick wank in the bushes and then I arranged to go round to his later for a proper bit of rumpy pumpy in the warm. Which I did. We had some couscous, some wine and a very nice bit of How's Your Father before I headed off back to work at the club.

Another time, drunk, I was lured (well.....) into the bushes by a young man who suddenly appeared out of the foliage, naked – he had a big cock so I was lost. I could have been murdered, right there, in the bushes, in the dark, in the open air. But I wasn't. I ended up fucking him up against a tree. Or was it the other way round? Lost in the mists of time and beer haze now, but it was up against a tree. Deffo.

Round about this time, while I was still Y(ish)F+S, we discovered 'Stallions', much to the dismay of my liver and my pay packet. This was located – long gone now, along with all these other places I have shared with you, so pivotal in creating this boy/man/homo – in an alley, Falconberg Court, behind the Astoria on Charing Cross Road, formerly known as BANGS! (Opposite Centre Point, where I used to wait, trembling for my Stevie....). It was open on Sunday afternoons, long before the licensing laws allowed alcohol so it was a 'Tea Dance'......hahhaaaaa. Was it buggery! Well, for two hours it was – actually sandwiches and tea, from 5 –7 but then, happy four hours began, two drinks for the price of one. Well, it was carnage, let me tell you.

During the sandwich hours, there would be played old tea-dance favourites and oddities like Eartha Kitt - *Old Fashioned Girl, Time Warp, Sweet Transvestite*, Liza, singing *New York, New York,* etc. it was so camp, and full of the weirdest people (we turned up on Fetish night once – we were up West and near, and just decided to pop in.....people being dragged around on their hands and knees, wearing jockstraps, or nothing, bollocks dangling, being slapped and spanked by the customers, as they stood idly drinking and chatting. People tied up to the pillars, facing inwards and having things inserted in to their arses, or forwards, cocks out for anyone who fancied it to have a go. I'm telling you – even I, after all I'd seen and done, was somewhat alarmed, mostly I think because it was straight and I felt really uncomfortable with straight sex, although it wasn't really sex per se. I don't really like having it rammed down my throat, you know. We stayed well out of the way, at the far end of the bar and ogled.) and it was the most unusual place – the pillars were like trees and they had fish tanks inserted in them. Truth.

B.O.G.O.F.!! Everyone got terribly, terribly drunk and made some bad decisions because of it. One night, in the toilets (which were always very busy, if you get me drift) I got...what's the word......waggled at by the bloke next to me. Beer goggles askew, I smiled at him and the next thing I knew, he had pushed me backwards in to the cubicle, I was down on my knees, amongst the condoms, used tissue and cum, sucking him off. You know, when the moment just takes you? Something you would never imagine in the daylit world, but filled to the brim with pints of Stella it suddenly seemed an OK thing to be doing. Until someone else, pissed or because the floor was a bit er.....slippy, fell against the door of the cubicle. Mr. Waggle hadn't locked it and, just as he'd shot his load over my shirt (I never swallow on the first date), the door flew open, knocked him against me just as I was cleaning him off, I did a bit of impromptu sword swallowing and was knocked backwards and I smacked my head against the toilet. It seems I was knocked out momentarily. Mr. Waggle just legged it and the next thing I remember was someone saying *"Its oright, e's breevin"*, and walking away again. Charming. A hand up would have been nice. Not very dignified, I sat up, covered in spunk and bits of tissue from the floor. Why was it always a debacle? Why did it always happen to me? I cleaned myself off as best I could, and went back out in to the bar.

"Where've you been?" asked Tony, now draped around a city type. *"I thought you only went for a wee."*

"I did, but .....I got.. er...side-tracked."

"You're SUCH a Trollop!" he squealed. *'You don't know the half of it,'* I thought but didn't elaborate. And so the evening passed. I ended up – or maybe that was a different Sunday – in someone's bed, miles and miles away, I had no idea where – nice man, nice shag – and then being dumped at some suburban railway the next morning as he, it being Monday, had to go to work. I got the bus home, stinking of fags, and stale beer, wondering my life had gone.

 It certainly wasn't supposed to be like this.....

Falconberg Court W1, the entrance to what used to be Stallions.

THREE.

Then, one Sunday, I met Edward. We were all shiny and clean, hair all Andrew Ridgelyed up, ironed tee-shirts, in fact I think this was the night I was wearing a vest – I could fit in one in those days – and we were all up for a bit of...well Tea Dancing. Juice and sandwiches first, then drinky – poohs. Nicky was on the Bacardi and cokes, Tony on the – God knows, gin probably, and I hit the Stella. Two for the price of one? It would've been rude not to.

Tony, Nicky and me, Stallions Tea Dance.

Dancing ensued. Twizzling round the tiny floor, sweating like a pig, wafting Aramis as I went, when BOOF! I smacked right in to a middle aged, blondish, non-descript bloke.....who had the hairiest chest I had ever seen.

Beer spilt, down both our tops – well, his shirt, my vest – expecting some kind of *"OI! You CAHNT! Watch where you're FACKIN going"* kind of thing, but what I got, over Jimmy wailing about sitting on the platform with everything he owned in a little black case, and the wind and the rain on his sad and lonely face, was:

"Sorry. Not looking where I was going. Crowded tonight eh?"

"Erm..Yes," I yelled in response. *"Sorry about your shirt."*

"It's just a shirt. It'll dry. Sorry about your vest...Shall we just take them off?"

And there we were, dear reader, topless in a gay bar! Just like Heaven, only with more fat. He was sweaty and all his chest hair was plastered to his skin, and he smelled...smelled proper manly.

'I'm never gonna dance again

Dum de dum de dum...

The way I danced with yoooooo'

...... wailed George, and Edward and I , for that was he, smooched and swayed, and slithered and snogged our way through the song that was to become 'OUR TOON' during our brief courtship. I loved the way he felt – he was stolid. That's a good word. STOLID. Not fat, not a 'chub', but solid and hairy and a very pleasant man, a sweetie, a kind man with a nice cock and a gentle way of making love to me. And a tendency for stalking, it turned out.

Amazingly, we didn't do IT that first night, but arranged to meet up the following Sunday, which we did. Same packed floor, same heat, smell of fags (as in cigarettes, obvs.) and beer, and gay boys wearing aftershave, me included. And there he was, smiling at the bar.

"Hello, hun," he said. *"I wasn't sure you'd come. I'm so pleased you did."* Awwww. That's nice eh?

"I said I would, and here I am." I think I was alone that week – Tony was IN LURRVE with his banker by this time and had no time for such lowly haunts, such hovels...

"I know, but that's often said. To me, anyway," and he looked so lonely for that moment and I was pleased I was not one of the ones who had let him down.

"Drink? I noticed you were on the Stella. At least, that's what you threw all over me last week!"

"Oh yes please. Lovely."

So we found a space to squeeze into and just talked; nothing heavy – work, hobbies, ex-boyfriends, what food we liked.....chat, a bit of touchy feely when the moment arose – a hand on the leg with a laugh, a touch of the hair to emphasise a point.....he was a very pleasant man, hairy and generous and mature and I liked him. So, when he said the immortal line: *'Do you want to come back to mine?'* it wasn't sleazy or cheap, it was a genuine invitation to make love with him and I accepted.

He didn't tell me he lived in St. Albans, mind you, so it was a bit of a late night, a whizzy – headed drive out of London, away from the city to the countryside. I was a bit pissed (no change there) but not drunk and I was really looking forward to what lay ahead. We arrived – a neat semi, in suburbia, exactly what one would have expected. A place where Ted (contractions, already!) lived his single life, wishing it otherwise and hopeful that tonight would change his life.

We had a gin and tonic; he'd not been drinking due to the drive home but we sat, I drank, had a St Moritz, the last legacy of You Know Who, and it all felt fine. *"Come on then,"* he said and took my hand and led me gently to the bedroom, leaving my gin and my cigarette, which rolled on to his Ercol coffee table and burned a hole before it went out. Seemed to be a habit...

We didn't just fuck, come, and go to sleep. He was very gentle, undressing me slowly, slowly so my excitement increased. He was expert – how did he learn these skills? – and once naked, he undressed too. He was very sexy; as I said, solid, well built, a little bit of a belly, but beautifully hairy and a nice fat cock, which was more than ready for the event. We moved on to the bed, and kissed and caressed each other, passed slowly through the stages and finally he fucked me, but oh! So gently, considerately, asking if it was OK, taking his time, taking care.

After we'd come, he took me to the bathroom and gently washed me clean in the shower, then himself and returned to the bed, and there we slept till dawn.

In the morning, he offered to drive me home, all the way back to Wanstead. Not really very keen on forking out whatever in bus and train fares, I agreed, and off we went. Big mistake.

'When two tribes go to war....

blaring from the car radio, Ted's hand resting gently on my knee, occasionally moving up to affectionately rub the back of my neck. We arrived back at the Flats and we parked up and, checking there was no one around, he pulled me to him and kissed me. In public! I nearly died! It was a bit exciting, rebellious though and I didn't pull away.

"OK, week's work coming up. Next Sunday, Stallions?"

"Yeah, sure. Thanks for a nice time. Really."

It had done me good, as it goes – after the trauma and grief of the parting with Ken and nothing else other than casual, drunken sex, mostly with strangers and always without joy. The pleasure of that lasted as long as the ejaculation, then just emptiness again. So Ted was nice, it was loving love making, caring and comforting.

He drove away.

Tony, who was at home, went *"OOOOOOOOH Nigel's got a boyfriend..."* or something equally wanky and I told him to fuck off, but smiling in that secret way that new lovers have.

"He's quite nice, ACTUALLY. He takes care of me."

"Loaded, is he? Nice car...."

"I don't fucking know! We shagged. I didn't ask him how big his bank balance is! Anyway, YOU can talk. How is Quentin or Rupert or Tristram, or whatever his name is? Got into his wallet as well as has pants, have we?"

"No need to be such a bitchy queen. I was only 'avin a giraffe."

"Tony, you are the LAST person who should be using rhyming slang. You sound like Katie Boyle. Polari, maybe, but not slang. It doesn't become you."

"It's Barry, actually. But it isn't going anywhere. I think I might go to Amsterdam." Which, in fact, some while later he did. But I'd moved (again) so there was nothing binding us together.

Back to now:

"Ted. He's called Ted. Well, Edward actually. Teddy. Teddy Edward. Ha!" and that's what we called him from then on. *"We're meeting again next week, down Stallions. Fancy it?"*

"Maybe. See how it goes. I didn't vader his eek. Has he got a bona cory?"

"Actually, don't do Polari either. You sound like a knob. Leave it to Julian and Sandy."

"Who?"

"Never mind. And yes. Quite bona. Not that it's any of your business."

"Are you in luuuurve?"

Oh FUCK OFF!! No, I'm not. I've only known him 5 minutes." There was a glow, however, that little tickly thing that hatches in your belly and flutters and wimbles about when you think of them. And yet.....yet....there was something not quite right.....

Great in bed, nice body, fun to have around, kind, generous......and yet.....

Anyway, the week passed. More shifts at the Club, drinking too much, ignoring Rod when he came in - that way madness lies – or, more specifically, as I was also part time DJ (well, the bloke who just put the records on the crappy old deck that was balanced precariously over the sink), playing Michael Jackson's *'One Day In Your Life':*

> *'One day in your life.....*
>
> *.......You'll remember me somehow*
>
> *Though you don't need me now......*
>
> *I will stay in your heart ...And when things fall apart*
>
> *You'll remember one day......'*

....yeah you BASTARD!! HAHAHAH. See? Serves you right.....I don't know if he heard the song, listened to what it said, heard what I was saying, or even gave a flying fuck. All I know is that it gave ME great satisfaction, in a petty, jilted sort of way. You see, dear reader....I STILL wasn't cured....

The week passed, the club full of the usual crowd.....

......Les, known as *'The Duchess'* who, after a few pints, would always excuse himself, climbing elegantly down from his stool to *"go and spread me tired old cunt lips over the lavvie."*

.......And Ian, as usual, discovering last night's (or last week's, it had been known) uneaten kebab still all wrapped up in his Parka pocket, or not wrapped and his pocket full of chilli sauce and shredded lettuce. He's chuck it in the bin, then replace that night with another, pissed, with the munchies, thinking *'Oooh I could go a kebab now'* and then deciding to have it when he got home. Or not.

......and Jean and Lola, the tallest and smallest lesbian pair you ever saw; Lola, 5 foot nothing and Spanish, with a Latin temper to match and Jean, about 6 foot 4, but devoted to each other. Lola loved Jean even more than the slot machine, into which she would feed a week's wages at a time, swearing and kicking it when it didn't pay out. When it did, she bought drinks, when it didn't she turned into Angry Woman. Gill, who happened to be up staying one week, happened to be passing the machine Lola had just left, and dropped a random 10p in and won the £100 jackpot. Senorita Lola was *muy muy enojado*, fucking FURIOUS, judging by the looks of pure hatred directed at my hapless sister, and the string of Catalan expletives that poured from her mouth.

.......And Rita. Glamorous Rita, who in all the time I knew her, never ever bought herself a drink, but was always supplied with copious amounts of brandy and soda; once, she was so pissed, we went next door to Paki Jim's (don't gasp – it was the 80s) and attempting to get something from the freezer, she just overbalanced and slid, gracefully – always gracefully – head first in to the freezer, and lay nestled amongst the peas and broccoli florets until we had stopped laughing enough to pull her out. Another time, at a party, I watched her tip, in slow motion, sideways into a fishpond. When she was dragged out, dripping slime and water from her astrakhan coat, they asked if she was OK.

"Of course Darling, But I need a brandy."

"What do you want with it?"

"Oh, I'll have another brandy." Ah Rita. Rita, you were a star, one of the old school, fag hag extraordinaire, and dead now. But not really, not really dead because here she is, on these pages, and in my heart.

......John and Carlos, the most mismatched lovers I have ever met. Carlos, he from Barthelona, and John from Befnal Green – I have never seen two people who should never have met. As barman, I would be left alone whilst a war broke out above our heads. Before the 'top bar' and restaurant, (in which I wined and dined Miss Diana Dors; oh yes, people – I mixed with the stars! Lynne Perry came to do cabaret once too (God, what a filthy mouth SHE had!) and 'that Olive from '*On The Buses*', (as John proudly referred to Anna Karen) was opened, and it was still being used as a storeroom, they used to go and fight up there. I mean PROPER fight – there would be ice buckets hurled, glasses smashed, stacks of table overturned – I would go up to fetch something and there they'd be, shirts ripped, bloody....then they'd reappear and carry on as normal. It became SO normal, punters took no notice of the thunder above their heads; I just turned the music up.

The week passed. We didn't open Sundays then so I was free to go and meet Teddy Edward. And there he'd be, all clean, and tidy, freshly pressed shirt, and open smile.

"Hello darling!" he'd say. "Stella?"

"Don't call me Stella!" I'd say, and we'd both laugh.

It certainly made a change from buying Chris beer all night. I hardly saw him much now - he and Vince were on a completely different merry go round these days – off to the bondage bars, the dark rooms, the S+M scene.

"Hi, Yes please," and the evening would begin – pleasant, nice, easy and somehow, 'Careless Whisper' would always be played, as if they knew, and there we'd be, chest to chest, slippery, slick and randy. Back to St. Albans, hand in my pants now, caressing me, making me hard, as we raced along Edgeware Rd and out of the city, back to suburbia and to sex behind the nets.

The next day we went to the city. I was sitting on a large stone, just outside the abbey, when he came up and leant in really close. "I love you," he said. "I really love you. You have to move in."

And at that moment, something clicked in my head. Something just wasn't right......I saw he was a bit...creepy, a bit axe murderery......

"Well, I don't think we should rush, Eddie. We haven't known each other long and...."

"No, no, you must move in. We should be together. We are meant to be."

"Well, maybe in a bit. What about my job?"

"I have a job. A good job. I can look after you."

"But you'll be at work all day. What will I do?" (stuck out here in lace curtain land, with no friends or anyone I knew...)

"You can stay home and wait for me and then we can fuck all evening if you like. I know how you like it..."

Suddenly I didn't. I looked up at the abbey, 'There's no comfort in the truth, Pain is all you'll find' ran through my head (cheers, George!) and realised I was quite a long way from home here, and totally reliant on Teddy Edward to get me there.

• • •

"Ted, can we go? Umm.....Only its Tony's birthday and he's off to Amsterdam soon, so I would quite like to spend the evening at the house. Sorry, I forgot about it....."

"But I want you to stay here. It's Sunday. It's what we do...."

"Yes, but......"

"No buts, Darling. We stay here. Let's go home now. I'll make you a big gin and tonic."

I looked up at St. Alban, asking him for some guidance, but he just stared off into the middle distance, as he had for the last thousand years, and was no bleddy help at all. So we left the now quite welcome safety of the crowds and went back to what had instantly in my head become The Bates Motel. After a couple of gins, which ironed out some of the anxieties, things felt a bit better. He kept coming over and cuddling me, reassuring me that we would be very happy here and going back to the kitchen to do the dinner. We ate, I drank gin, smoked a few fags (for me nerves) and everything appeared as normal. Except......except...I couldn't UN hear his voice back at the Abbey, the calm certainty of his plans. I drank gin. Then he was beside me.

"I love you. I have never felt like this before. Sex is just out of this world, and you do fancy me, don't you. My hairy chest, my fat cock. Don't you? We can be together, here or anywhere you want. Just don't leave me."

"But Ted, I have a job and I like it and.... and anyway I have paid Bruna for this month so really I have to ......"

"You don't love me do you? I'm not good enough. I thought you fancied me...."

"I DO. I do, but it's all a bit fast." (I hadn't told him about Rod or Ken, all still a bit raw, to be honest) *"Can we just slow down a bit?"*

"Sorry. Yes. Sorry. It's just that I have never met anyone like you and I want to spend my life with you."

Oh fuck. Now what?

"Let's go to bed shall we?" The gin had numbed the pain and I could work out what to do tomorrow.

"Yes, darling, come on," and we went to the bedroom where once more, he undressed me, gentle as you like and then fucked me senseless. No, wait...that was the gin.

The next morning was work for him (you know, I NEVER did know what he did or where he did it) so up we got, and back to Wanstead, where he dropped me, after a kiss.

I went indoors, and raced upstairs, to Tony's room.

"Tone! TONY! We have a problem. I think he's a fuckin NUTTER. Nice and everything, but a bit meshugena."

"Why? What's happened?"

"Well.....nothing. But......I think he might be a serial killer. Or something."

"YOU'RE the fucking nutter....he's a lovely bloke."

"Hmmm. Well......."

"Come on, let's go out. Let's go to the Royal Oak for a change. They're open."

So we did, and a few beers took away the panic.

The next morning, I got up, to go the club for the morning's bottling up and.....there was his fucking car! Parked in Ingatestone Road, the cheeky fucker. Round the corner. Just sat there. Then he drove off. OH MY GOD!! He's stalking me!!

"TONY TONY!! QUICK!!! TEDDY EDWARD. HE WAS THERE. IN HIS CAR. ON INGATSTONE ROAD. RIGHT OPPOSITE!"

"Fer fuck's sake. There's no one there."

"THERE!! IT WAS HIM. I KNOW THE CAR. HE'S SHAGGED ME IN IT!" (I hadn't gone into detail about that, in case you thought I was trollop. But he had).

"God, you're a trollop," said Tony. *"What was it like?"*

"IT DOESN'T MATTER WHAT IT WAS LIKE! WHAT MATTERS IS THAT HE WAS HERE. OUTSIDE. JUST.....JUST...STARING!"

"Oh well, he's gone now. What time is it? Let's go down the pub."

● ● ●
108

Busman's holiday. Nice one. But we went and it was fun. If you like drinking in a pub where everybody stares at you, like in *'An American Werewolf In London'*.

"What did we come in here for? Remind me?"

"To stop you freaking out. Anyway, I'm off to Amsterdam. LEKKER!"

"When?"

"Weekend."

Oh, Tone. Gonna miss you, you tart." And if we hadn't been in The Holly Tree, I would have kissed him. But we were. So I just gave him a slap on the back.

"Oooh! Butch! Come on, let's get out of here!"

A couple of days later, we were sitting down to tea. Bruna had just emptied the pepper pot on to her meal – I have never seen anything like it. A layer, an inch deep, of ground black pepper on whatever we were eating – and I'd gone to the kitchen to refill it, when the phone rang.

"It's for you," said Tony. He put his hand over the mouthpiece and said, *"It's him. Teddy Edward."*

"Tell him I'm not here, you idiot!"

"He says he's not here. I mean, he's not here," said Tony. He turned to me. *"He says he wants to meet you for a drink. What shall I say?"*

"Tell him I'll call him. When I get in."

"He says he'll call you when he gets in. ....Ok, bye."

"I don't fucking believe you. You just...oh never mind. How did he get this number?"

"Oh I gave it to him. He was outside in his car yesterday, and he looked so sad and he asked if you were here but you weren't so I gave him the number."

"WHAAAAAAT? YOU DID WHAT? YOU FUCKING FUCKING IDIOTIC FUCK!" (There WAS some advantage of having worked at PPR) *"Brilliant. Just fucking BRILLIANT."*

The phone rang.

Tony picked it up again. *"Oh hello again. Hmmm. Yes. Hmmm. Mmm. Ok. Bye."*

"That was him. He's in the phone box on the corner of Dames Road, and he says there's a little club on the High Road and he'll wait for you there."

"Well, I obviously can't go can I?"

"Why not?"

"Fer fuck's sake Tony. What do you mean why not? How can I? And anyway, it's Selina's and I can't meet him there…!"

"Why not?"

"Because…well, because…..just BECAUSE."

"I'll come with you."

"I. AM. NOT. GOING".

"Poof."

I ignored that, and went to my room. I couldn't go THERE, of all places. I didn't want him to know I knew everyone there, and it was my local. I decided to ignore it.

But, every night – must be after work? Maybe he WORKED near? I don't know – I never did find out – every night, there he was, parked up in his car, in Ingatestone Road, opposite the house, so he could see the front door. I took to sneaking in the back, down the little ginnel that ran between the houses. Why I didn't just go over and speak to the man I don't know, just say Hi and ask why he was there?

"Tony. TONY! YOU go out and talk to him. Go on. PLEEEESE?"

"Erm…OK. What do I say?"

"Well, just say……Nigel thinks you're a really nice guy but he doesn't want a relationship now because he's really really upset about his last boyfriend. Or something. Use your imagination!"

"Right."

A few minutes later he came back.

"Well? What did he say? What did you say?"

"He says he'll meet you in The Holly Tree in ten minutes."

"WHAT?? You fucking idiot! What did you go and say that for?"

"He looked sad. And he was nice. Oh, and he's got his shirt open a bit. Just in case. You know what you're like and so does he, obviously. HAHAHAHAAAA!"

Dilemma. What to do, what to do? If I DON'T go, he'll keep stalking me, or worse, but if I DO go it might give the wrong signal.....

Well at least the Holly Tree is a public space.........so, I got my coat and off I went, across the Flats, not feeling very confident, past the tree where I got shagged (or did the shagging – I STILL can't remember) and up to the pub door.

Just as I was about to push it open, a hand fell on my shoulder......OMIGOD OMIGOD I'm being murdered or raped or dismembered or worse, right outside the pub. I turned, and it was Tony!

"YOU CUNT!! YOU FUCKING SCARED THE SHIT OUT OF ME, YOU FUCKIN FUCK!" (thanks, again, PPR)

"Oh I thought you could do with some moral support. Did I make you jump?"

"Yes you fucking DID!" but I was secretly pleased to see him.

We pushed open the door, and there was Teddy Edward, sitting at the bar. With my pint. Of Stella. Hunnnngggggggggg.....

"Hello darling," he said. *"I got your favourite."* This was getting seriously weird now, and I was glad of Tony's support.

"Oh, thanks. You remember Tony, don't you? From Stallions?"

"Oh yes. Why is he here? I thought I was just meeting you so we could decide what to do. I've missed you."

We sat, I picked up my pint and, downing in almost in one, beer cascading down my chin and coat, and I said, *"Look, The thing is Ted. Er, Edward...I....."*

"OK, look, Tedward. He doesn't want to be with you. He loves your hairy chest, a lot and you've got a beautiful cock, - he told me all about it – (Actually I hadn't but I let that pass in the splendour of the moment) - but that just ain't enough. He thinks you're a weird stalker and he wants you to leave him alone or he will call the police and tell them you raped him. Or something. Oh, and not that you asked, you dry lunch cunt, I don't want a drink. Come on." And he took the pint glass from my hand, closed my astonished mouth and led me out the pub.

● ● ●

"OH, and don't try following ME, because I'm going to Amsterdam."

Outside, after I'd managed to regain my composure, from the shock of what just happened, I said,

"'Dry lunch cunt'? Where did you pick that up? That was brilliant!"

"Oh, something Rod says. He said it one night when we were out".

"Out? OUT?? You out with Rod???? You fucking….."

"Calm down! No don't worry, I didn't! He's old enough to be my Dad!"

"I didn't think you did. It's nothing to do with me, who you shag. (Please, not him…)Anyway - that was brilliant! Do you think it worked?"

"Hope so 'cos I won't be here to look after you…"

"TONE! I love you!!" And I gave him a great big kiss, right there, outside the Holly Tree, Wanstead, E11!

I never saw Teddy Edward again. And, Ted, if you're reading this, as unlikely as that may be, sorry I burnt your coffee table, your chest IS beautiful, as is your todger, but….you were just too much. So, sorry. And thanks.

Round about this time, John , at the club, decided to open an antiques shop, a couple of doors down from Selina's, in an empty shop. He filled it with junk, put outrageous prices on everything and then sat amongst the clutter like Miss. Havisham. Only with a moustache. He didn't sell anything, as I recall, but it was a diversion as he and Carlos were finally parting, before either of them was indicted for murder. John was having to divide his time now between the club and the shop, as Carlos kept disappearing off back to Spain (the 'why' was revealed later) and was short staffed, so he offered me a job in the shop. As I was single (again) and free to choose, I accepted and so become Sales Manager of 'John Jack's' Shit Emporium. I didn't sell anything either, though it was quite a sociable thing, people in and out, saying *"HOW much? Fuck off…."* and *'This is a load of old crap"* and other compliments, but not buying. And so the days passed, I, like Albert Steptoe, sat amongst the de-feathered stuffed birds, old candlesticks with chips on the rims, blackened saucepans and sideboards with knobs missing. There was a tiny toilet, where I used to hide when Carlos came in to have rant about something he couldn't find in the flat or he needed some money, and a small back room where I could go and have my lunch, on the old musty bed that was there, behind the curtain.

* * *

In the evenings I still worked the bar, even the new upstairs one, on the street level. Selina's had come out, she was out and proud, even with the doors open on to the street so people could hurl abuse without having the trouble of going down the back stairs to the cellar. We even had a doorman, gentle Ben, whose wife was very understanding about why her husband wanted to spend every evening with a load of lairy poofs, who made us all feel safe and protected from the big bad world outside. There was also a swanky new restaurant attached, at the back, through the bar, so we had a chef and at some point, Nicky had reappeared and she was waiting tables. Somehow, John managed to get Diana Dors to come and eat there, and I was invited – a more down to earth lady you couldn't wish to meet. John was in full gear, full of pride, full of shit, but very proud. He'd built this club (as he would drunkenly tell us every fucking night, downstairs....*"Boys and gels..."* he'd go, and everyone would raise their eyes to heaven, saying *'here we go again'*, *'yes we know'* and *'shut the fuck up'*, while he droned on about how proud he was to have the club and wot 'e 'ad done for us etc etc....), he'd got two bars AND a restaurant running and he had, although he was a total knob, done a good thing for us and I for one am grateful – it was the place that gave ME the courage to face who I was, to be welcomed in to a tribe and get proper shags, at last. I felt a part of a family, a group 'like me' who also *liked* me and that was a comforting thing. I realised just HOW alone I had been, spiritually and emotionally, with my background, my family and my neighbourhood. All of that was designed to make me conform to its norms and quite clearly I never would've been able to. I would have been one of those bitter, unfulfilled married men, fucking other men in secrecy and shame, never knowing the sense of freedom that being able to say (even if we didn't know the right words for how we felt) "I am gay, queer, a homo, a poof!" – whatever appellation suits – brought and I got that, slowly, *brick by brick, piece by piece, putting it together*, as Sondheim said, all those furtive college gropes, all those awful events involving cock and sorrow, all the pain caused by taunts and letters from those who were supposed to love me, led to this, this little haven, with Ben protecting me at the door and my friends and fuck buddies all around.

Peace in my heart.

FOUR

I don't know how it happened really. John and I became 'an item'. Yes, dear reader. ANOTHER boyfriend! Number four in this saga, this catalogue of disaster. La! So free with my favours......

As I say, I don't really know. What started off as a bit of a shag turned into BF and BF, and Runner of the Club to boot!

There I was, in John Jack's, selling jack shit, when John Jack came in to John Jack's and said, *"Sold anything?"*

"No," I said. *"A couple of asks, but the prices are too high for this erm..material."* It was junk, but he believed with all the acumen of Harold Steptoe, that it was all undiscovered treasure, invaluable if only the people who came in weren't so thick that they didn't know quality when they saw it.....

"Oh well. Lunch time. Did you bring anything? I can get the restaurant to rustle something up if you want?"

"Nah, its fine, I got sandwiches. I'll go out the back."

"Oooh, I could do with a sit down. Mind if I come?"

"Er..no. Its your shop..."

So we went out the back, and sat in the only place that didn't have piles of crap on it – the rickety old double bed. And, yes, we did. He suddenly leant in and kissed my ear (how quaint!), my cheek, my neck and then took my hand and placed it on his crotch.

How, you may say, do you remember events of nearly 30 years ago with such clarity? And my answer is that these 'incidents', recounted throughout this book, were IMPORTANT, formative, made me who I became finally; they were moments, some tiny and detailed and some momentous in their effect on me, that stuck in my head, like lyrics – I can recall whole songs that were current at those moments. When I hear them NOW, I can see where I was, what I was doing, who I was with, what I felt, what happened around that song in its time. I remember what people were wearing, what the weather was like......but I can't remember the number of my mobile phone. Go figure.

Anyway, back to the shop......the next thing, my tuna roll was on the floor and I was on my back, with John on top.

"I've always fancied you, you know, but you was always with someone. Rod, and that Ben, and Tony, and that Chris….."

"Hang on. Stop….. It was KEN, not Ben, I've never 'been with Tony', and certainly not Chris; he's my friend. Anyway, I didn't know you fancied me."

"That's cos I never said nuffin. But I did. And now you ain't wiv anyone so is it OK if I fuck you?" Who said romance was dead?

By now he was seriously up for it, straining in his jeans and to be honest, having caught sight of the hairs on his chest, so was I.

"Well, could we just……"

"Just what? You know you want to. You like it. Rod told me."

WHAT?? Fucking Hell Rodney………

"Well, I do, but, can't we just….have a wank or something this time? Maybe next time, when we know each other a bit better, we can…."

He'd undone his jeans by know and I could see his cock, and it was fucking ENORMOUS. Deffo attractive but enormous.

"I don't think that'll fit, John. It's rather…."

"Hnnnnngggggggggggg" groaned John as he came all over the bed and my jeans.

"Sorry. Bit quick, couldn't help it. Here, let me finish you off." (Who was it? Who said romance was dead?)

"OK, just let me get my jeans…."

Just then: *John? JOHN? You in there? I need to get into the flat. Are you there? I want the keys. Dios. Esta tienda está llena de mierda. Tú también lo estás..Madre de dios! This shop is full of shit and so are you."*

"Oh CHRIST!! It's Carlos. Quick, in to the toilet!" and he shoved me, jeans down, pants half off and erection flagging, across the little room in to the cubicle and pulled the door to.

"I'm in the back, just coming...... (no pun intended. Actually, John never did puns. Actually, he didn't do anything very funny I was to discover). *"I thought you were in Spain. You weren't due back till next week."*

"I know, but I ...needed something. Can I have the keys please? Why are you looking so red?"

"No reason. They're behind the bar. I'll come and get them."

And they went out. I could see through the crack on the door; John WAS looking rather flushed, as it happens. I waited for the 'Jing a ling a ling' of the little bell over the door to sound before I emerged, drying semen on jeans which were still at half-mast and I hadn't been able to move for fear of kicking the bucket. The mop bucket, I mean.

I didn't know, and neither did John at this point, that Carlos had cleared out all the business accounts, and had all the money transferred to Spain (*allegedly*; that was the goss) and had just come back to get some paperwork to do with the transfer. We also didn't know this was the last time anyone would see him for months. Rumour has it, he was seen last sitting on the wall of The Bell, opposite, staring at 'Dirty Nellie's', which was what Selina's had become not long after he'd gone. Mostly thanks to him.

But, for now, all was well. Peace reigned in the Club as the warring factions had gone their separate ways, or, at least Carlos had buggered off. No more fights, no more broken chairs and ripped tee shirts. John was happier, although upset – they'd been together for some time; in fact, just after the Club first opened.....but he was back to his big larger than life self – laughing too much, drinking too hard. We didn't mention the aborted shag; I just thought it was a one off, an attempt at a quick bit of some of the other, but I DID notice that John kept looking at me, being extra nice to me, giving me a drink *'on the ahse'*, in fact, several *'on the ahse'*, though not when anyone else was around. I do believe, dear reader, I was being WOOED! Or he was just trying to get me pissed all the time. Which worked, I should mention.

One night, we were all up in the top bar, chatting and being nice to each other, and someone handed John the newest edition Gay Times saying, *"Whoar! Look at him. There's an article about him. Have a look. Wot a knob! He is I mean. Look what 'e's done!"* John took the mag, went 'WHOAR' and proceeded to read the article, went 'WHOAR' again and gave it back.

"What do you think about THAT? Fuckin' twat, eh?"

● ● ●

116

"Yeah, yeah. What a twat!" said John, who then bent down to busy himself behind the bar, fetching up some refill fruit juice. Whoa......something wrong here.....not quite sure what.....

"Show us the mag? I haven't seen this month's." (Actually I'd never seen any month's. I think the last porn mag I'd seen was at ATC camp all those years back – I can still see those weird crevasses and folds.......).

I looked at the article in question - something about two 'lads' snogging on Oxford Street, outside Spats (oh the memories!) and then calling the copper a 'Fat Wanker' – and asked John, *"Have you been there, John?"*

"Where?"

"The club, in this article."

"Oh. No. I don't think so."

Do you know where it is?" I persisted.

"Oh, erm, yes.....no. I'm busy." And he left the bar and went off downstairs. Nope. Definitely, something not right here.

A couple of nights later, same scene. There was a paper on the bar ('EENIN STANNIT') and I passed it to him, pointing at an article. He took it and appeared to study it. Only, the paper was upside down. Fuck me! He couldn't read it. He had no idea.......Oh my god. HE CAN'T READ! Suddenly, many things, anomalies became clear – hesitations, excuses when I'd asked him to deal with an order, to read me something on a list, anger at being asked his opinions on something being talked about which he would have needed to have read to be able to give an opinion....the poor bastard was illiterate. My heart was suddenly filled with pity – no, not pity, sorrow. He'd endured this all his life and never once spoke of it.

It made sense now, all the bluster, all those *"Boys and gels, I made this club from nuffing. I came up froo the East End wivaht a pot ta piss in, an' I made this club what it is...."* speeches he would make and be endlessly mocked for were actually the only thing he had, the only proof that was, in his eyes, validation of himself as a person; he'd made a difference in spite of being so severely disabled in the world in which he found himself.

After this realisation, this brash, loud, foolish man seemed to me to be something brave, something powerful and I found myself defending him when other members were being less than kind *('Oh shut the fuck up, you old cunt. It's ONLY a gay bar'*, when in fact, I realised no, it was *far* more than that.) and found myself drawn to him, wanted to help him, wanted to make it better. He seemed to me, now, someone who'd faced massive prejudice all his life, all 55 years of it – he was illiterate, queer and Jewish (though not completely, if you get my drift.... Ha ha) and had had to hide all of those things, and still, in spite of all of that, he'd opened this little bar, this Saving Grace, and had, I believed now, every right to be so proud of it. Yes he WAS annoying, yes he was a twat but still – I was drawn to this man and slowly, slowly, we became 'an item', though one that was to be kept secret, for some reason.

John and me, just before it all went wrong...

I now worked full time behind the bar, became 'manager' (for what it was worth. Nothing, actually) and my popularity suddenly both soared and plummeted – soared because, in my largesse, I was able to give people one *'on the ahse'* whenever I felt like it, Lady Bountiful, me, and everyone suddenly seemed to be my best friend (I knew it wasn't real, but it felt nice) I was able to play what music I liked too, as Carlos was no longer DJ (if ever there was a misnomer, a crappy old record deck, balanced over the glass washer and a pile of out of date records, was it. DJ, indeed!) Anyway, OUT went The Ovaltineys:

We're happy girls and Boys!'

Yeah, thanks for that.) and in came Feargal Sharkey, Level 42 and Talking Heads. I had the 'budget' for the records and I was in control!! HAHAHAHAAAA! A touch of 'Big Yellow Taxi' here, (she was still my companion in times good and bad), a smidge of Marc Bolan and 'Ballroom of Mars' there.....I learned too that if they didn't like the music, they came off the floor and back to the bar, to drink and eat the 'free' peanuts which made them thirstier. A little track from Bowie's 'Lodger' – nothing like 'African Night Flight' to get 'em flocking to the pumps! – or a soupcon of Sade's 'Your Love is King' to kill the night stone dead....I was, let's face it, shite at the job – I played exactly what I liked (and usually no-one else did, ignoring the calls of "WHAT THE FUCK IS THIS???", "PLAY SOMETHING DECENT, YOU POOF" and "CAN WE HAVE SOMETHING WE KNOW, PLEASE?" etc etc) and gave drinks away like they were going out of fashion (which of course, they never would). It was Chris – remember him? The Wise Man. The Saviour – who, one night said,

"You're going to ruin this club. Play music people actually LIKE, so they want to come here! They don't want to hear fuckin Moany Joni or fuckin wanky Mark Bowler..."

"It's BOLAN, actually..."

"I don't care who he is! Play something we can dance to. Fill the floor, make us hot and thirsty, and make us have FUN! It's like a fuckin morgue in here. AND STOP GIVING AWAY FREE DRINKS!! They don't really like you (ouch) they just know you're good for a bevvy. Use your fuckin nut. It's a business, not a charity."

I knew he was right. Again.

"OK no need to shout. I got a bit carried away."

"Alright. Good. Put on that Bowie thing – F F F F FASHION – we like that. Mine's a lager. Cheers. OH, and I know you're shagging John."

"How? It's a secret..."

Maybe if you stopped playing that...that Laura Brannigan song and making eyes at each other....'Silent Partners'. Pffft. Make it a bit more obvious, why don't you?"

He didn't miss a trick. And neither, it seemed, had anyone else.

"Shagging John then? Carlos has only been gone five minutes," said Gloria. "Mind you, I never liked him, smarmy dago cunt. Mines a Bacardi..."

"Gotta charge for drinks now, Glor. It's a business you know."

"Yeah well, start after me."

That night, after downstairs had closed, and we were seeing off the stragglers out of the top bar, we sat down and I said:

"Look, John, I've been a bit of a knob. Sorry about the music. And the free bevvies. I just got a bit carried away."

"It's alright. I just love having you around. I didn't want to spoil your fun. Yeah, night Ben. Thanks. See you tomorrow."

And then it was just we two. Without going into too much detail, I will say only this: Red banquette, large gin and a re-enactment of 'Last Tango in Paris', as the restaurant kitchen was just along the corridor and there was no time to go upstairs.....

At this point, mostly because of the 'mistake' I'd made one night at Bruna's, I was about to be made homeless. Honestly....you'd think I'd murdered a baby or something. What happened was we'd all gone to Stallions and got wazzed and got kebabs and got the night bus home but Nicky had lost her keys or something so I said she could sleep in my bed and I would share with Tony. Poor Tony, who hadn't come with us that night, was fast asleep and awoke to find his friend stinking of fags and beer climbing into bed with him.

"What the FUCK....???"

"SHHHHHH NICKY HAS LOST HER KEY. HE CAME WITH ME. SHE DID A WEEE... THAT RHYMES....HAHAHAHHAHA."

"Shut up, you idiot. You'll wake the girls."

"OH. OK. SORRY. SHE DIDN'T DO A WEE. WE HAD A KEBAB. IT WAS NICE. I DON'T WANT TO SHAG YOU IN CASE YOU'RE WONDERING....!

"Stop shouting. STOP. Go to sleep."

So I did.

In the morning there was a shriek. *"WHO ARE YOU????"*

Bruna had gone to my room, alarm call as usual, to find a complete stranger in my bed. With a cold kebab.

"Oh, sorry. Nigel said it's be OK. I lost my key...."

"Right. That's fine. You'd better go now though. And take your kebab. Thankyou."

I looked at Tony. The icy calm of Bruna's voice hadn't sounded normal and I feared the worst.

At tea, there was a thunderous silence at the table. No conversation, no sound other than that of Bruna smothering her food in pepper. A thousand years passed.

"We're thinking of decorating your room and using it for a storeroom for my stage outfits," said Bruna, in to the void.

"Oh. That's me fucked then."

"I'm afraid so…you can stay till the end of the week if you like."

Like, six days? Brilliant. Now what.

I know! I'll get Gill to move to London and we can share a flat!

And so it came to pass.

We had to borrow the money for a deposit off my Dad, who was only too willing to lend it (though he never EVER let us forget it) because, I am assuming, he thought that living with Gill would get me away from all those predatory homos, out of the Den of Vice and it would give her a chance to entice me to leave the SSU and his son would be normal and acceptable again. He would be able to hold his head high as I would be delivered from the Devil.

It didn't, as you can imagine, quite work out like that.

I travelled down to Cornwall and helped her pack her stuff into a rented van, up to the roof and in to the remaining space we squeezed the drugged and very resistant cat and set off…..away, away back to London, to the smoke and the lights – to a new chapter for me, a new life for Gill and my parents waving us off, with different agendas – my Mother wishing it was her, and my Father full of hope that his son would now be saved.

It was the journey from hell. It rained. And it rained. Then it rained some more. It was dark, the night only illuminated by the oncoming headlights of massive lorries. We just drove, and drove, eager to get there, aware of how far we had to go. At one point the cat seemed to need a pee so we pulled over onto the hard shoulder, somewhere along the M4, and tried to get the lead attached to the cat which by this time was no longer drugged and was having none of it. We pulled the poor little fucker out of his box, from whence he had lain for, what – five hours now, and attaching some string to his collar, put him on the roadside, on the hard shoulder.

 "WEE! Go on, WEE!" said Gill. The cat, traumatised, drugged , wet and with his fur blown in the opposite direction by the draft of the massive lorries screaming by not three feet away, covering us all in spray, was not really in an ablutionary mode, it seemed.

"WEEEEE! FER FUCK'S SAKE CAT...WEEEEE. I'M GETTING DROWNED HERE!" But, no. Nothing. Just a plaintive whine, which probably translated something like: "I'm not going to wee. PUT ME BACK IN THE VAN OUT OF THE RAIN AWAY FROM THOSE FUCKING HUGE LORRIES THAT MAKE MY EARS BLEED. I DON'T KNOW WHERE I AM, WHERE I AM GOING, BUT BY BASTET AND ALL THE GODS OF EGYPT, WHERE I WAS CONSIDERED IMPORTANT, I WILL GET YOU FOR THIS. I WILL FIND THE RIGHT TIME AND RIP OUT YOUR THROATS. YOU BASTARDS." Or something.

"He's not going to is he?" I said. "Can we go now?"

"OK. Please himself," and Gill picked him up and put him back in his basket. We had no inkling of his plans.

We drove on, mile after mile. I knew East London, where Forest Gate is, and was none too pleased that the poxy landlord wouldn't meet us there, but insisted we went to his place. North of Edgware. The complete opposite direction. It was late, it was dark and still it rained and this would add at least another two hours to the trip. We eventually arrived at his address, and refused, out of pique, to rub his mezuzah. For those of you who believe in Divine retribution, this turned out to be a mistake.

He was an odious little man, with an equally horrid wife. He was short and fat and he smelled, sour, cigarry and with halitosis that could've stunned a horse. We went into their Parlour - his word, not mine – and said,

"This is my wife. She annoyed that you're so late. All the shops are shut. Never mind, bubbeleh," he said to his equally monstrous wife, all fur and no knickers, "and you all dressed up and farpitzs."

"We couldn't help it, you know. We've driven about 400 miles as it is and if you'd met us in Forest Gate, it would've been two hours earlier and the shops would have still been open!"

• • •

I wasn't as you know, prone to outbursts, but I was tired and this little fat fuck was just about the end......

"FEH!" said Mrs. Fagin. "I'm not one to kvetch, but Harrods is at LEAST an hour's drive and I've been waiting FOR EVER. I was hoping for a little metsiah, a little bargain, but it's probably too late now."

I couldn't believe my ears!! We'd driven all this way, in the worst of conditions and all this, , this SHLUB, this nagging, irritating old bag can do is dare to moan because she can't to fucking HARRODS to spend OUR money???? Well KISS MY TOCHES!!!

"Just hand over the money, so we can go," said Gill. And we watched him count it out. Ten by ten, all the way up to £600. Deposit and a month's rent on our new life. And so SHE could go to Harrods the next day for a bargain. Mazel Tov. You arse.

When we got there, over to East London, eventually, with the cat now howling pitifully from the rear, probably with a bladder the size of Kent, we walked in, using the key that Fagin had so generously handed us, to find the flat damp, musty and with all the furniture in the 'furnished flat' all stacked up against the walls – beds included. We could've cried, and probably did.

We spent our first night, huddled up on a mattress on the floor. And the cat did a shit in the hall.

It took us some while to get the place straight. The gas boiler was faulty – we know this because Gill found me almost unconscious in the bath the first day we used it. This meant we had to call Fagin over to see to it and....it was a strict NO PETS policy. So, the poor cat was unceremoniously flung out the back door whilst he was there, with both Gill and me ignoring the wailing coming from outside.

That fixed, the furniture, such as it was (the lying bastard) all in place, we alternated between Selina's and the flat as I was still working, and still shagging John of course. We landlords take our work very seriously you know. Within a few days, Gill was offered a job as in the restaurant as Chef, as the other one had left the same time as Carlos did because she'd not been paid for weeks. Unfortunately there were no customers, so she only cooked a meal or two, and mighty fine they were too being that she is actually a trained chef. John still paid her though, which was nice of him since it was becoming increasingly clear that we were in trouble financially.

One day I volunteered to give him a hand with the books, so with

'In a West End town, a dead end world,

The East End boys and West End girls

tootling on in the background, I sat in the restaurant 'in an East End Town' and opened the books for 'Selina's Inc.' Jesus H Christ, on a bike! What hieroglyph was this?

It wasn't this obviously, but it might as well have been. Nothing, and I mean, NOTHING, had been accounted for; nothing had a date, the figures didn't tally.....I am no book keeper but even dopey me could see things weren't erm....quite right.....

"Ummm. John? Can I speak to you for a minute?"

"Sure. Is it about the books?"

"Ummm..yeeeeessss. I don't think they're in a very good state..."

"Probably not. Carlos dealt with all that side of things....."

I know WHY, of course as John couldn't read at all or write particularly well either, but...for fuck's sake! This was utter chaos.

"Well, where's the bit that says how much money there is in the bank?"

"Dunno."

"Well, where's the bit where it says what we have to pay out and what we're getting in from the bars and the restaurant?"

"Dunno. There?" and he poked a finger hopefully at some random column and it was at that point that I realised WHY Bassy the chef hadn't been paid for weeks, WHY the brewery weren't going to deliver at the weekend, WHY John was taking money straight out of the till to pay random tradesmen who came aggressively in the bar, and WHY, most of all, WHY Carlos had gone. Carlos had had gone and SO HAD ALL THE FUCKING MONEY!!!

He KNEW John would have no clue as to what was going on in the books, with the paperwork, the wages, with the credit and debit...and he stole the fucking lot, probably transferring it to a bank in Spain, gradually, so nobody would notice. The bastard. The conniving thieving greasy arsed BASTARD. Was this the reason for all the rows? Did John know? Surely not, as he didn't seem to understand why his suppliers weren't.....supplying. I knew. I knew it was because they hadn't been paid. Because that fucking dago had been syphoning all the money to Espana. What to do? If I tell him, there'll be a 'Kicking in' chairs and some knocking down tables, in a restaurant in an East End town'.......

....Shut UP Neil Tennant, let me think. And my decision has been my secret to keep all these years. I told him that we, the club that is, just wasn't making enough money any more. Not that his lover had knicked everything, stolen all that he'd worked to achieve (*"Boys and gels...."*) and was now the architect of his demise and despair. Probably best – I'd seen him when he was angry and I didn't like it.....

"You know what it's like, John. New bar opens, all the queens go WHOOOOO and run off there. No loyalty, just the chance of some better lighting, newer music and someone they might not have shagged yet. They'll be back, when they're bored of Benjy's, Harpoon Louis, The Playpen, the Pink Panther...they're all poncey. And expensive. And people have to travel.....It'll be OK. You've got REGULARS......"

Actually they were no longer quite so regular, and they became even less regular when we found ourselves without any beer. In a bar. We had resorted to me going up the road to the Offie, to buy cans of lager, with my tartan wheelie shopping trolley (oh the SHAME!) and flogging 'em for a quid a go – we had to raise enough cash to buy the same again for the next day plus to try to save a bit to pay the looming bills and, in my case, being very keen not to have my knees caps shot off by one of the blokes John had 'dunn a bit 'o business wiv'. Gradually, and I don't blame them for I would have done the same, loyalty or not, people began to question why they would pay a quid for a can of lager they could get next door in Paki Jim's for 26p. Chris was first to complain (no change there then) and he caught the mood of the people (all 4 or 5 of them) when he said:

"A quid. A QUID? For a can of lager? I ain't paying that! Fuckin' ridiculous. Come on Vince, let's go somewhere we can get a proper pint." And they left. And sadly so did everyone else, over the next few days and weeks until we had no customers at all, and no way to keep the wolves from the door, and the kind of wolves John 'ad dunn a bit 'o business wiv' should be kept from one's door at all costs.

As all this was going on, Gill and I were still living in Forest gate, chucking the poor cat out every time Fagin, as we now liked to call him, came round for his rent or to fix the huge number of things that were shit and didn't work..... *"Yes ACTUALLY, you DO need to have boiler fixed or get done for manslaughter"*....

....*"Ooooh! Look! There's that really annoying stray cat again Gill. I wish it would stop coming into our garden all the time. It's very annoying. It poos in our garden. Honestly, the neighbours should keep it in or something"*.....

...and generally realising that, though we loved each other dearly, and she was working at the club (I say 'working', but really just sitting round with us, and getting paid for nothing) but she'd met someone back in Cornwall just before we'd decided to set up home together, and of course, I was now getting a regular doses of John's appendage (we'd sorted out the issue of 'accommodation'. All along, it was just practice!) which was quite a powerful draw; Gill had been home a couple of times to see him and it was becoming clear she wanted to be with HIM, not here, with a leaky boiler and the cat pissing all over the cover of my 'ALF' LP.

So, after not very long, it was decided that we'd admit that we both needed shagging on a more permanent basis and to hand in our notice.

Once it was decided, it was obvious that after I would move into the flat upstairs with John. It was a bit sad, after all the trouble we'd gone to, not to mention the bound – to- be never ending comments from Pater about how generous he'd been (check), how he'd hoped it would work out but once again his kids had let him down (check); about how we'd never repay him but that was OK because he loved us and would never mention it again which as you can imagine was absolutely not the case. And of course, Gill hadn't managed to save me from damnation. Hey ho.

Anyway, just before she was due to leave, John decided to treat us to a night out at the theatre and got tickets for '*Evita*' at The Prince Edward Theatre, UP WEST!! Oooooh went the two Cornish peasants, and not without reason; though I'd been in London for some years now, I'd not been to the theatre very often…..

…one notable exception to that was one night when I was still at Pearcroft Road, and Chris and I had gone to the Salisbury (like some crack whore, unable to resist) and he, of course had copped off and left me. Again. HOWEVER, this night, I was schmoozed by a very nice gentleman:

"*Hello there. Erm..Hi!*" he said. Oh myyyyy – A Southern Irish accent. I was done for…Yes, YES!! I'll do whatever you want…..

"*Hi,*" I said. Here we go again. Two 'Hi's' and the deal is done.

"*Alone you are? I tought I saw you wit someone?*"

"*I was. Now I'm not.*"

"*OK. That's good news, so it is.*" (*He probably didn't say that, but I'm just trying to build up the picture. Please read all his lines like Paddy O'Flaherty). "*Well, I would like to buy you a drink* (Mine's a lager!.., something I would later regret as I had to push past a whole row of tutting people as I needed a piss and couldn't make it to the interval. Should've had a half.) *and then go home with you, so I would, but, I have two tickets for 'Romeo and Juliet' at the Aldwych for tonight if you'd like to go. First. Then I'll follow you home on me bike, so I will.* (Really? I could live in Reading, for all you know!)

But, the voice unmanned me, the Shakespeare enthralled me and the chance of a shag after decided me.

"*Yes! And Yes!*" I said.

So that's what we did:

Had a drink, saw a play and then shagged. A very nice night thankyou, Christopher Hartley – if you hadn't buggered off, Seamus (*not really) wouldn't have come over and…..

I digress….

So we borrowed John's vegetable van (Used for delivering them, not MADE of them. Honestly…..) which had two front sliding doors neither of which worked unfortunately and were jammed open, and it blew PLUMES of black exhaust, leaving both of us doubtful we'd get from Leytonstone to Forest Gate and back at all.

However, it didn't let us down, so there we were, all glammed up, Gill wearing a FABULOUS black evening gown and me in a suit, tightly belted in in order not to fall out of the cab of the van through the open doors as it went round corners and we farted and belched our way across Wanstead Flats, like a scene from *'The Grapes of Wrath'* only with Ma Joad slightly better attired. And no alfalfa sprouts.

There was a cab waiting and off we swished, heading up West. The show was stunning, but even better and more memorable was the end of the evening when Gill made THE most spectacular entrance you could wish for, to lock away in your box of 'The Funniest Things Ever'.

John and I were down in the foyer, with all the luvvies, going *"Mahvellous Dahling. Mwah mwah"* and *"That Laney, you know, Laney Paige. Mahvellous....."* when all of a sudden, my sister came into sight, careering, nay HURTLING down the curved stairs from the Circle, people flying for their lives, or getting knocked out of the way as she careered past. Apparently, she'd caught her heel in the hem of her dress and stumbled forward from the top step and hurtled like an Exocet missile down the stairs, furiously flapping her black dress as she went, unable to regain her balance or stop, gathering speed and squealing like a squealing thing as she went, down in to the foyer, people scattering and leaping out of her way until she glided, ladylike, to a halt in front of John and me.

"Ah!" she said, not missing a beat. *"There you are."* Cool as. Utterly brilliant.

Fagin was less than pleased when he came round to return our deposit as we weren't going to stay on the extra month but threatened instead to tell the council about his British Gas Death Trap.

"Shnorrers, both of you, Spongers! Thieves!" he said. *"Bubeleh was right about you. And YOU!"* he said, pointing at me - *"Faigelah! HOMO PERSON!! And YOU!"* pointing at a very bewildered Gill, who had not had the benefit of living with Rod and having heard all this Yiddish before, *"YOU – are probably a nafka!!* ("He's calling you a whore," *I whispered) "MOMZERS!!* ("Now he's calling us bastards! Good job I listened to Rod, eh?" I said.)

"OY YOY YOY!! Out of my house!!"

This was rapidly turning into a scene from *'Fiddler on the Roof'* – any minute he was going to break into *'If I Was A Rich Man'* and start 'Deedle deedle deedle deedle dum' –ing all over the place until, that is, the cat arrived, pissed on Alison Moyet, again, strolled around the room and then nonchalantly swaggered out of the open front door, with a 'FUCK YOU' look, that only cats can do.

At this point, we thought we were dead, well and truly busted and deposit-less but instead, he yelled something unintelligible both in fury and in Yiddish and *THREW* £300 at us, up in to the air, notes flying around and falling through the air like in one of those gangster movies, only we didn't get riddled with bullets at the end.

"MEESA MASHEENA AF DEER! I WISH YOU A HORRIBLE DEATH!!" he bellowed and just turned around and stormed out. Result! Money and still alive!

"Well," I said. *"That went well".*

So, Gill went home, and I moved into the Club, now a shadow of its former self. No money, no punters and an increasingly drunken Landlord.

To cut a long story short, in which nothing much happened, we had to sell up to the first buyers, and as the club was in so much debt, we came away with….nothing. Selina's became 'Dirty Nellie's' and an era came sadly to an end. All those faces; all those loves, tears, fights, hopes, laughs…..where did we all scatter? Who survived the War? Who married as soon as we were allowed to? Who died? Who went to foreign shores? That parade of shared hearts and minds and cocks, all passing through this little world created here, here among the brickbats and arrows of the East End when we thought that none of us even deserved such a thing.

It all happened very quickly. The two guard dogs, Sebastian (too savage) and Bruno (too old) had to be destroyed and we suddenly found ourselves in the Housing Office for Waltham Forest, with 2 suitcases, 3 cats in boxes, 2 Shih Tzus, a Mynah Bird and a Great Dane pup (don't ask…..John was offered it, 'cheap like', and he thought I'd like it. In another life, it might have been a good idea….), refusing to leave until they found us somewhere to live. Probably due to the fact that Lena and Prince wouldn't stop barking and trying to bite anyone who came near, they found us somewhere pretty quickly – a one bedroom flat, in Walthamstow, in a block right next to the pub, which according to Google Maps, has ceased to exist, so I can't give you the name….

And so we moved. All of us. Plus the furniture from the club. Freddy, who CONSTANTLY yelled, *"QUITE NICE!!!!"* was on the kitchen window sill, the dogs were wherever they could fit in, and then Lena had pups. The place stank of ammonia and birdshit, dog farts and cat piss, and we weaved amongst the huge antique (fake) buffets, climbed over clothes, tripped over animals and each other...it was fucking CHAOS!

John decided to 'go back to his roops', as he put it (never having seen the word) and got himself a pitch on Walfumstow Market, selling pet food. He got a little van and off he went, early each morning to set up, to *yell "NOT FREE PAHND! NOT TWO PAHND! WHO WILL GIVE ME A PAHND FOR THESE LAHVELY CUTTLEFISH? YER BAHDGIE WILL LAV YOU FOR EVVA! FREE PAHND OF BONIO FOR A PAHND. YER DOG WILL LAV YOU FOR EVVA..."* etc etc, on and on, all day, wind or shine, until packing up time when he'd load it all back in the van, his life measured out not in coffee spoons, but in packets of Trill and hide pig's ears, come home and more and more frequently, go straight out the back in to the pub, from where he'd emerge, red and angry and on the verge of doing me harm. Luckily, he had the oil painting of his Muvva on the wall so he would sink to his knees in front of it and sob and sob until I gently, like a child or a wounded bird, led him to bed, where he would fall into healing sleep, to begin again the following day. *"ONLY A PAHND, MISSIS. YER CAT WILL LAHV YOU FOR EVVA....."*

I meanwhile, also unable to stay in the menagerie we called home, with its stink and hairs and puppy shit, decided to go back to teaching. Yes, dear reader, the very thing I said I would never do, in ANY circumstance, for ANY reason, having HAD IT with education and shitty jam jar hurling kids, I was desperate to return to as it was my only skillset and means of escape from that flat. John came home at lunchtime to see to poor Sam, the Dane, who was growing still (but who by now I absolutely adored), to let him out in to the tiny garden and I signed on with the Supply Pool and ventured back into the classroom.

Dear Sam, way too big for this life....

I struck gold, as it happens. My first job was in Chingford, for a week. Someone had gone off sick, and it turned into two weeks then three and then I was offered, subject to interview, the job full time. Hmmmm.... what to do? Sit at home with Freddy shrieking *'QUITE NICE'* without a break and stepping on dog turds? Go and stand at 'John Jack's' and sell millet sprays for budgies, OR......get the fuck out of there, earn a decent salary and have some social interaction with people who knew stuff about STUFF. John's range of interests, and therefore conversation, was quite limited, to say the least. I had begun to wonder why I was there at all – or had been, in the first place. Was it because I'd felt sorry for him? Because I would be running 'my own' club? Because he had a gorgeous cock and was always keen to use it? Probably all of those things, in the beginning – great sex, a bit of glamour and free beer. But it would not sustain.

So, I took the job. Mr Lucky's back in da house!

John was not so thrilled. In fact he was livid.

"Who would look after the animals?" Erm...YOUR animals, actually. *"Who would cook tea?"*

"Well, YOU. Or we can share it.......OK, I'll cook tea (you fucking BLOKE) *but it will have to wait until I get home and sometimes, I'll be late. Rehearsals, or staff meetings and stuff."* (I didn't elaborate on the 'stuff' but, dear reader, if you promise not to let it go any further, I will tell you: I was having an affair. With a LAYDEE! Tell you more in a bit.....)

"Well, I can go to the pub until you get home."

This turned out to be a singularly BAD idea, and often I'd have to go in and get him, and he'd be slumped in a corner, pissed and sad, or all revved up. On those occasions, he'd go on and on, pint waiting for when I arrived to make me stay (regardless of any food I'd been preparing) I'd have a drink with him and then he'd think it was OK to take me home, all 10 yards of it, across the car park, past the cockle and whelk van – who said romance was dead? - and in through the back gate of the flats and try to shag me. I say 'try'. It usually ended up with him either losing his stiffy or his temper, neither of which was conducive to shagging. I preferred the first of those two scenaria; at least he'd then fall off me and then asleep, rather than the other option which usually involved him in screaming at me about the Club folding (like it was MY fault!), about Carlos leaving him (like it was MY fault!), about not being able to read (like it was MY fault!), about everybody treating him like a cunt (like it was MY fault!) and he wished his Muvva was still alive….the abuse would turn to tears and then we'd have a session of him kneeling in front of her portrait, now hanging in the hall, sobbing and wishing he was dead.

His Yiddische Mamma…

I would watch this scene with conflicting emotions: on one hand, I would feel desperately sad for him, all his dreams in tatters and his celebrity gone or, on the other, I wished he WOULD SHUT THE FUCK UP AND GO TO BED. And, no Freddie, it is NOT *"QUITE NICE"* so you can shut the feck up as well.

So, this was my world. Full of cat hair, dog shit and vitriol.

Or, half of it was. The other half, almost like some kind of secret life or a parallel universe, was full of creativity, and inventiveness (this was before the National Curriculum and the carnage that Kenneth Baker wrought) and interesting people. I was staying on late at school, partly due to planning and marking (funny how you get back on the bike, seamlessly) but also the less time I spent with Mad John in the Crazy House the better. I was growing again, the kids watering me, and nourishing my spirit.

And there was Miss….and, you know what, I really CAN'T remember her name – that's awful, eh? …. But let's just call her Sue. She was very beautiful, with the most amazing hair and open ready smile, and a wonderful lilting Welsh accent. And fabulous tits.

Now, dear reader, I haven't been able to explain this to myself, and as nobody (except, now, you) has ever known about this, I have had no one to talk to about it, to rationalise it. But. It happened. We had a fling, a 'do', an affair, a tryst. We crept out of school into the pub, The County Arms, on the corner, where we would hold hands under the table, or sit side by side and I would stroke her neck whilst pressing our hips together. It was the behaviour of teenagers, but utterly transporting. I was aching for her, and the fact I was a poof never came into the equation. We would write each other notes, staple them closed and send them next door with a child; *"Could you just pop this next door to Miss, Jason?"* Jason, the least likely to open it, would go next door and in a few moments would return with a reply, agreeing that she's quite like it if I masturbated over her tits, but only if she could suck me off on a bus. Triple staples.

I don't know if the other staff knew; probably they did, as we behaved irrationally and giggled together like fools, brushing against each other in corridors easily wide enough to pass in; I would use her to 'demonstrate' dance positions, holding her waist, her arms, her legs, drinking in the scent of her, as the kids looked on in rehearsals for a re-enactment of the Blue Bag thing I'd done back at Balls Park (BALLS PARK!! BALLS!! SIR, YOU SWEARED!!). We went together to lunch, went to get anything needed for school, took any chance to be in each other's company. Was it love? It was certainly lust, but, I hear you say – she has all the wrong bits for you. We've all read what you get up to, what you like, so…..? All I know is that back at her flat, with hubby late home, we snogged and I fondled her boobs like a good 'un and eventually, pressed for time, shot my load in my jeans as I humped between her open legs as she sprawled backwards on the stairs, leaving a wet patch on her crotch. Now, YOU explain this. I can't. It was utterly wonderful though and yet somehow, I must have justified it by saying it can't be real because I am in the SSU, and my history, laid out in these pages, would suggest otherwise. So was it OK? No, of course not. She was married and torn by her behaviour. I was with someone too (whatever that meant) and we were both unavailable and from different species. Maybe SHE too justified it to herself by saying that I was a homosexual and so no real threat to her marriage. Erm...You have a wet patch in your crotch, made by my semen – I think that's quite a weird one to explain to hubby though: 'Oh it's OK, he's a poof!' I don't think that's gonna go, somehow. That though, was the apogee of our...our....whatever it was. I think we were quite frightened by the red intensity of that encounter; aware that maybe, had there been more time, I would actually have fucked her, crossed the Rubicon, from where there would have been no going back; I couldn't have unfucked her and the consequences of that moment became clear to us both. So, somehow, we sort of smiled ruefully and walked away; she began looking for other jobs and we behaved like normal people around each other. I can still feel the bones of her pelvis, though, as she ground against me. How strange, after all these years.

Then, one day, a normal day, a day of Maffs n Spellin, a day of packed lunch and Banda machining, the secretary came to me and said, *"You had a phone call. Can you meet your friend in The County Arms for a drink at lunch time?"* Really? It was a Thursday; we only went down to the pub on a Friday... What friend? Well, that wasn't too hard to guess as since leaving Selina's. I hadn't seen anyone apart from Chris and Vince – I wasn't allowed out much you see – so it must be them. Odd. *"OK. Thanks. Right, you lot - Number 10. DEFINITE. And be careful with the ending..."*

One day. A normal day.

12.00 came, the kids went out, I managed to get someone to swap canteen duty and headed off down the road.

One day. A normal day and there they were, the only customers, three fresh pints on the table. Quiet. Something in the air...

"Fuck me! Don't tell me you bought your own? Wonders'll never.....

"Hello," said Chris. *"I've got AIDS".*

....and a FUNERAL.

I felt like I'd been kicked in the chest, like I was doubled over, no air, unable to catch my breath. The blood was banging in my ears, I was spinning, falling, over and over, down to some alternate Wonderland where what he'd just said would make sense.

There was a silence of a thousand years, and into the silence I said: *"What do you mean? What kind of AIDS?"*

"Don't be a cunt all your life. AIDS. There's only one sort of AIDS. Well, there's hearing aids but they don't have capital letters and they don't kill you. AIDS. AIDS. AIDS, as in: I'm dying. I wanted you to be the first to know."

An honour, a bitter bitter gift.

"How do you know? Are you sure? They might be wrong. They might've...."

"Look," he said, and knelt in front of me, there in The County Arms, in the bar where so much joy had been had. Gently taking my hand, he said, *"They're not wrong. I've had several tests and it's quite advanced so I don't know how much more time I have. I came here to tell you, my oldest, my loyalist, my oldest and twattiest best friend, so that maybe we could spend some time together. Not seen much of you lately what with that old cunt you're living with and me being in bed quite a lot. You reckon you can spare me some time? Now that I don't have much of it left? Eh?"*

I looked at him now and could see the grey pallor, the gauntness of his features; I hadn't noticed it before, but then, I hadn't seen him for weeks. I felt shame, self-loathing and utter utter desolation. Not Chris. Not my angel, the man who'd guided me away from disaster after disaster. Who would guide me now? Not my Chris, who'd got me into the most awful trouble, who'd made me so furious I could've stabbed him, who'd made me laugh so hard I thought I would choke. How would I manage?

I looked across at Vince, a man I didn't know too well, and he was sitting there, as still as stone, agony etched into his features, giving his beloved man this moment of reconciliation, the first stage in a long long farewell, preparing his friend for an inevitable tragedy, one that was being played out all over London and beyond, but knowing that this, this was the only one that mattered.

"Yes. OK," was all I could manage.

"Drink up then!" and he downed his lager in the time honoured way, as if he hadn't just said what he had, as if time had rewound itself and there we were, down the pub.

"I need a wazz," he said and stood up to go to the loo. *"Mine's a lager."* A little unsteady, a little light, the beginnings of his wasting away.

"He's pretty sick, Nige," said Vince. *"I don't know why he's not contacted you before now, but it was his decision to make. I guess he just wanted to be sure there was no exit. He's been on this new thing, AZT, but it hasn't worked, so he will die, sooner rather than later now. He's getting sicker. He's been to hospital twice with PCP and his CD4 count is nearing zero. You read the news, you know what's what. All you can do is give him some of your time, and love him. He's always calling you a twat but I know there's no one he loves more. I'm really sorry it has come to this, but you must know how hard this was for him today. He's being his usual gobby self, but he's terrified. Not of dying but of the manner of – it can be pretty grim. So please. Please just be there for him and see if you can…..*

"What are you two fucking talking about? Got yer knitting out have you? Les tricoteuses who haven't even got the bevvies in. I hope it was about me. As Oscar Wilde once notably said: 'If there's one thing worse than being talked about, it's…

"…..NOT being talked about," we chorused dismally.

I went to the bar.

When I came back, I realised that forty five minutes had passed and I was feeling a bit pissed (being Chris, the first pint was Stella, and I'd had no lunch. Hurrrrrrr.) And you know what? The art lesson I had planned for that afternoon now seemed a teensy bit irrelevant. How could I go back, smile at the kiddies, smelling of beer and on the edge of tears and talk about Seurat in order to facilitate a lesson on pointillism? I couldn't. My friend, my dear terrified friend, was dying, before my eyes, and whatever consequence of my next action would be was not as important as that. I went back to the bar, borrowed the phone, rang school, told them I'd received some terrible news and I wouldn't be back that afternoon. I hung up before I was asked any questions, ordered three more pints of Stella and returned to the table.

● ● ●

"Come on then you fucking lightweights. Beer." And I drank to drown my sorrows and all those that were to come.

That evening, when I eventually got back, John was already asleep in the lounge, drunk and sad. I had nothing to say but went to bed, where he joined me at some point later and woke me. We lay there in the dark. I searched for his hand and said,

"Chris is dying."

Sleepily he replied, *"Never mind. We'll talk about it tomorrow."*

"I want to talk about it NOW please. He's dying. He's got AIDS."

John sat up and put on the light.

"How do you know?"

"Because he TOLD me. How do you think I fucking know?"

"Oh well. He was always shaggin' around. Not surprised really. Pity though, eh, him being your friend and all that. You haven't shagged him have you?"

"NO I FUCKING HAVEN'T!! DON'T WORRY YOURSELF."

Selfish bastard, but actually I knew he was right to ask. The demon was in our midst. The war was coming to our door, and striking us down. I suddenly was aware that it wasn't that surprising that Chris had become infected – he was, indeed, 'always shagging around', and his 'proclivities' were somewhat extreme. He and Vince regularly went to The Chain Locker, The Colherne, and the Mineshaft where the hankies were most definitely on show, and Chris had a veritable rainbow in his list of preferences - dark blue, light blue, grey and red. He'd also gone to Amsterdam for a weekend of 'Beer, Bondage and Buggery' with an American serviceman he'd been having sex with. You can imagine what went on; at least, he came back with a smile, and a sore arse. And, he believed, HIV.

I DID begin to make time for him, to make up for lost days, lost hours. I went to Leytonstone Tube rather than Blackhorse Lane; went to Burghley Road instead of to home. John got more and more angry; I got more and more determined to be the best man I could for my friend, and John could go fuck himself if he neither liked it nor understood. We argued, I stood steady, whilst not neglecting my 'wifely duties'. He would never come with me, would never involve himself in what was happening in that house – Chris was someone he'd known for years and I found it hard to understand or forgive him for his disinterest and pettiness about stuff – having to clean the flat more, having to cook after selling *'dahn the market all bleedin' day'*. And I could understand that, I could, but I needed HIM to understand that I needed to be with my friend, whilst I still could be. John had no knowledge of our history, our long years together, of the deep and abiding love we had and so failed to grasp the significance of what was happening, and happening to ME as well.

Those few brief months passed too soon. I met John Adams and Steve Reich, Terry Riley and Michael Nyman, Gavin Bryars and Philip Glass – they would fill the lounge with their insistent throbbing tones, while Chris would sit motionless, listening with his musician's sensibilities and would visit places in his mind only we could guess at. Even now, *'Different Trains'* takes me back to that room, that driving rhythm, *'one of the fastest trains'*, *'The crack train from New York'*.......maybe he was wishing he was on that train, *'From Chicago to New York'*, taking him away from here, from this room, from this speeding death.

We smoked, we drank copiously – the answer for us, for that time WAS to be found in the bottom of the bottle; it made things funnier, blurred, unreal for those few precious hours. But as those days passed, so did the time we had remaining to us. There were constant phone calls from sobbing lovers who had lost their dear ones to this war, this enemy we were fighting but with no weapons; Tony, Mike, Harry – all gone, all wiped away, wasted to nothing, rotted, sometimes blind, dementing as the virus attacked the very thing that made them who they were; these calls from these screaming wailing men made us all too aware that Chris was soon to be added to the list of the lost. As he comforted his grieving friends with words that could not soothe, he heard his own death rattle down the telephone line.

We went down to 'Dirty Nellie's', once and once only – too painful to return – but mostly we stayed in. His only other outings were to Barts, only to have the boxes of his demise ticked off, one by one. Another bout of PCP, a throat infection, peripheral neuropathy – the troops were mustering, calling him home, and his flares of anger – at us, at his sickness, at the world, began to subside to resignation and he spent more and more time in bed and I was going less often, partly as there was little I could do, partly because I felt it was important for he and Vince to have some time, such little time, but mostly because it was so agonising to see this man, that I had loved dearly, sworn at, adored, bought endless pints for, my Wilfred Weed becoming nothing. No life left. Smaller and smaller he became, and more ready to leave.

One Sunday, I was at home listening to John moaning about something and the phone rang.

"Nige, its Vince. Chris is back in Barts, the PCP has come back. Could you come?"

"Of course. Half an hour, tube depending."

"You can't go out, dinner's nearly ready," said John.

"I'll see you later. I have to go."

"You spend too much time with those two."

"SHUT UP YOU SELFISH OLD CUNT. SHOVE YOUR DINNER UP YOUR ASS."

And I left.

At the hospital, Vince was waiting outside the room.

"It's bad this time."

"Can I go in?"

"Yes, but I think he's asleep."

There lay my friend. Thin and grey and small, tubes everywhere like some monstrous anemone and machines whirring and beeping. My friend, who, I could see, was not long for this world.

Suddenly he opened his eyes and looked straight at me and said, in barely a whisper,

"Oh it's you. You're a cunt." And then laughed, but it ended up as a fit of coughing and gasping, so bad the nurse had to come and do something; I don't know what, as I'd been ushered out and was standing next to Vince.

"Thanks for coming. He asked for you." And then he just crumpled, slid down the wall and lay in a sobbing heap on the floor of the corridor.

"It's OK, mate. Well, it's not OK, but you know what I mean."

"I won't have a life without him. Who will look after ME?" and he sobbed and sobbed, like he had lost everything in his world.

I realised what he'd said.

"Oh fuck, no. Not you too?"

● ● ●
139

He just nodded dumbly.

Just then the nurse came out.

"He wants to see you. And DON'T wind him up."

I went in. He was breathing normally again.

"No," I said. *"You're a cunt. A cunt for doing this. A cunt for getting sick. And a CUNT for leaving us."*

"Stop swearing. I find it offensive. Don't cunt me, you cunt. I need a wazz," and he started to get up. He got to sitting, paused, turned to me, held out his skinny, tube-laden arms and said,

"I'm so sorry, about all this."

And I hugged him, so thin, so light, ephemeral, a man of no substance at all.

What could I say? Not much, really, as by this time, the lump in my throat was the size of the world.

"Help me to the bog?"

And he struggled to standing and shuffled towards the door, a man of 110 years old. *"And get me fags out of the drawer. I think Vince smuggled some in."*

"FAGS? You're not supposed to smoke! You've got PCP for Chrissakes!"

"Oh shut up you twat. What difference is it going to make?"

We shuffled across the corridor, his drip stand swaying, to the toilet, where he disappeared. Next we heard what would have been a shout if he'd had the breath: *I CAN'T GET UP! I'M STUCK ON THE BOG!*

We went into the toilets and there he was, door open as he hadn't been able to manoeuvre the drip stand in as well, pyjamas round his ankles, unable to find the strength to rise. In another world, a world full of light and joy, it would have been hilarious. But it wasn't it. It was sad and heart breaking and just another indignity.

We squeezed in, Vince and I, and pulled him upright.

"And don't be looking at my cock. We're not at Balls Park now, you tart."

• • •

Gallows humour of the blackest hue. And memory laden, with love and courage and making the best of a situation worse than any I could have imagined.

We got him back in to the corridor and he croaked,

"Vince, get me a chair? I want to sit out here for a bit."

It was the end of visiting, almost and my heart could stand no more for this session.

"Look," I said. *"I'm fucking off now. I'll try to get back tomorrow."*

"Fuckin good job. You were getting on me tits," he croaked. *"And if you're going to the pub when you get home, say hello to that old cunt you live with and thank him 'for all he dun for us boys and gels'. And have one on me. Mine's a lager. Don't start fuckin moanin. It's the last one. Think of the money you'll save. You always were a tight – arsed cunt".*

And of course he was right. The last time I'd buy him a lager, and he wouldn't be there to drink and then piss off to the bog when it was his round.

"John says to say….."

"No, he didn't but thanks for the thought. Now fuck off. You twat. Twatty cunt. Hahahaa, he gurgled, and then he lit a fag. Right there, where he sat.

"PUT THAT OUT!!!" shouted the Nurse. So he just threw it in the bin hanging on the wall beside him

I began walking away down the slope of the corridor and when I got to the door, I turned back, like Lot, and I could see him, sitting in his chair, and billowing out of the bin were plumes of black smoke just as he'd set the bin on fire in Wakefield Road, in our teacher's flat, back when the world was kind and funny and not fucked up, (no firemen this time) and he was looking at me, looking at me and laughing, through the glue in his lungs that was consuming his very life. Laughing, laughing.

That image is what stays with me. Not the shrunken hollow man he'd become but the laughing rebel, wreathed in smoke from the burning waste bin. Class.

I rang from home; a couple of pints later and he'd gone. Just like that. He'd gone back to bed and with Vince lying on the bed, entwined, beside him, he breathed his last breath and was no more. So that had been my last sight. Oh! Clever Chris – his last gift was one of comedy and irreverence not a dreadful bedside gurgling departure. He'd seen me and had given himself permission to go. That thought sustained me in all the bleak months and years to come, when I could really REALLY have done with him to stop me fucking up, which I did with ineffable style in the future that was mine to come. Without him in it.

In 'Old Friends', by Paul Simon, there's a line about being old and sharing a park bench and saying how strange it would be to be 70. We liked that song.

He said once that that'd be us, but that we'd have to take our teeth out to give blow jobs. But it wasn't to be; the promise couldn't be kept. I'm so sorry.

The funeral took place on the 17th October, 1987. We'd had massive problems with all the local undertakers as their pall – bearing staff all refused to carry Chris's coffin unless they could wear rubber gloves and masks. Yes, dear reader, this is the truth. All the ones in the area made the same stipulation and in all of those offices, Vince, like a smoter of vermin, said: *'WELL YOU CAN ALL GO AND FUCK YOURSELVES. I WILL BE WRITING TO THE PRESS ABOUT THIS, YOU BUNCH OF IGNORANT CUNTS'*, before going around the corner and sobbing in my arms.

In the end we reached an agreement with one firm that they would supply the cars for free (funny how the threat of a bit of bad publicity changes people's minds) and we would carry the coffin. Vince, me and four of their friends who were still fit enough, did the honours. As we brought the coffin out of the house, they took great delight in telling the Director, in his black hat and tails, and his *cronies 'LOOK OUT!! WE'VE ALL GOT AIDS, YOU KNOW!! ALL OF US!!'* and watching the ignorant terror in their faces. Anyway, Chris was stowed in the back, mourners were in the cars and off we went and oh! What sweet revenge! It was the day after the Great Storm, October 16th '87 and the road all the way across the Flats was strewn with broken branches, all of which the Mute, the arrogant cunt, had to stop, bend, and pick up and move as we proceeded. HA HA HAAAAA!! This meant it took AGES, and he would have been late for his next job. What was that quaking? Oh, yes – that would have been Chris, laughing his bollocks off in the back.

The funeral passed in a blur. Julie was there, but there was little to say – this was the man who'd stolen her life away, and yet here she was. All I remember is that on the flowers that John and I (he had also deigned to attend) had brought was attached a label, with our (my) message of condolence. And in inside the little bag were some coins: three 10s, a 5p, and 2p and a 1/2p. You bastard!!!! When we lived together, centuries ago, one of us has spilt beer on the electric fire and the element had blown. The new one cost 75p and he'd paid for it, and forever after, drunk, as a joke, or in anger, he would say, *"You owe me 37 $^{1/2}$p for the element."* I'd always promised I'd pay but never did and it became our standing joke. So, I thought as a final and irrevocable joke, I'd put it in the envelope and it would be burned with him as the coffin was burned. But no. The ushers had collected all the bouquets and there it was – the money, NOT paid back after all, so he could tell all the angels what a tight arsed cunt I was. As I say – class.

We went sadly back to Burghley Road, to a house less full, a house stripped of its power, for the 'do', which, given the circumstances went from sombre (most of the guests were facing the same future) to euphoric (from a sense of relief that all the pain was done, the event went off smoothly and there was no more to be done.) There was one table of food, and about eight tables of drink, probably on Chris' instructions. We all stood around, awkwardly for a while until the alcohol hit our bloodstream and forced the sadness out, at least for now.

"Shall we go?" said John. *"I've had enough and I have to drive."*

"Go on then," I replied, gin fuelled and manic, *"I'm staying. I promised I'd look after Vince."*

Without argument, for once, maybe recognising both the importance of the event and the fact that he'd be wasting his breath, he left. No goodbyes, no words of thanks or comfort. Fuck off then. And I returned to the bar.

In the front room, Vince was surrounded by his friends, a group I was no part of. A special, select group who all shared something so intimate, so indivisible, that it was 'members only'. The one thing that bound them, made them close, made them stronger was the one thing that would kill them all. And, to offset this fact, they drank, and drank and shouted LIFE! to the skies above; raised their paper cups to each other and to an enemy they could not vanquish. 'L'CHAIM' to their shrinking world.

Seeing that Vince was (for now) OK, I returned to the kitchen for more alcohol.

"Hi," he said. *"I'm Bill. A friend of Vince."* Middle aged, cropped hair, firm body, nice packet etc etc....all taken in in an instant.

"Oh, hi. I'm a friend of Chris. Was a.....".

Two 'Hi's'. Contract made.

"Must've been popular. Good turnout..."

"Yes, he was. I will miss him; he was a very special man" I said, but I wasn't really listening as, gin addled, my attention was now fully on the hair that was poking out of the neck of his shirt. There was that silence where the things that needed to be thought were thought, and then we looked at each other and Bill said, *"OK. Come on."*

We went upstairs, and we fucked. In Chris' bed. A Funeral Fuck. A Fuck for the Fallen. It was beautiful, it was sweaty and hard, he was as beautiful undressed as clothed, and it was redemptive. Covered in sweat and cum, we lay gasping, and smiling, with Chris looking down and saying: *"Nice one!"* I felt no guilt, no shame, only that somehow it was the only thing that would have made this shitty shitty day right. Gin and cock. It worked.

We returned to the party. Many people had left, others were unconscious, and there sat Vince, drunk and alone, more alone that he even knew yet. He saw me, saw Bill, nodded, smiled a small smile and raised a thumb. A benediction and a recognition that life goes on – people will still fuck, drink, cook and toil, and somehow, so would he.

He did. I know he found another soul to love; comforting and a solace but never a replacement for Christopher Hartley, drink blagger extraordinaire and all round wonder. Vince lived for some years more, doing good work, buddying the infected, nursing the dying until he too succumbed in April 1992. Five years of living, but only half living as his reason for being had gone. The piano silent and unplayed now, gathering to it the motes of dust in the sun coming through the unopened curtains.

Where did they go, those lovers, each at their separate hour? Where is the sheet music, marked and scored in pencil as he composed? Where are the Steve Reich LPs, the steel pistons they proudly used as ash trays? Where are the Doc Martins (18 lacers), the camouflage trousers, the love letters, the handcuffs? Who has them? Who has kept these doomed boys alive? Me. Chris lives on in this story and in the mug he made standing on my desk holding my pens. In the photos of Wilfred Weed and the drunken poems he wrote and I keep in my trunk and my heart. And Vince lives on in the letters he wrote to me after Chris left us and his heart was so broken the pages are stained with his tears. And in this poem he wrote when he thought he'd never rise again.

● ● ●

'Soft, For the Music Dies.'

Soft, for the music dies within this room
Where once the bridge that Heaven sings
to man, returning him to grace,
is an empty space.
Soft, for music never silenced never can return
and we the living must, its passing mourn
sighing in the gloom.

Soft, still within the silence lives the love
he crafted here upon an earthly stave;
the song, moon slivered nights and sunscaped days.
Soft, threading memory stakes the muted claim
which we, the living, tearful, bear the blame
denial of our grave.

Soft. Dying music's timbre strikes the note
discordant; chaos bring the age of truth
to him; returns all harmony and places times innocence.
Soft, here lies the living ache, seek the dawn of melodies.
Each day his love reborn sustains undying hopes.

Vince Lively, January 1988.

I wish I had written this, this elegy, which conveys the desolation and sorrow in the lack of music and love which had sustained them both. But I didn't. Poor desolate wandering Vince did, and I include it as a tribute to him and to my dear dear friend who had left us both.

Chris was gone. Bill drove me home, asked if we could meet again because the sex was awesome and I was a really nice man....but of course I said no. I had John, I had my job, the animals, the flat....it was a tempting but completely unreal thought – yes! Run away with this sexy sexy man and not have to think about any of that stuff! Go! GO! But of course, the reality was that no matter how gorgeous he was, how beautiful were his cock and chest and eyes, that fuck was just medicine and a final goodbye to my best friend in a weird kind of homage – life goes on in the face of death and it was necessary to prove it to myself.

I thanked him, kissed him gently goodbye, knowing somehow it was a goodbye pretty much to everything. He drove away, and left me standing on the corner of Pretoria Avenue and the rest of my life.

It became crystal clear, in an instant. As the car drove away, with it went the last thing connecting me to this place.

What did I know? What did I know that I didn't know 12 years before, when all bright eyed and bushy tailed, full of testosterone and hope, with my gal on mah arm, I arrived in London?

I know that the streets are not paved with gold. They are strewn with shit; broken hearts, rubbish boyfriends, (well, not rubbish boyfriends – it was just ME that was rubbish at HAVING one. Or four.), failed employment, dying young men, and a dead friend, for a start. I thought the years had been kind but when I kaleidoscoped them all together, it had all been pretty fucked up. And now, with the last thread cut, and turned to ash, there was nothing to keep me here. I didn't care what John wanted to do – he could come or stay. I wasn't even sure why we were together – feeling sorry for him because he couldn't read and his dago boyfriend had chawed all his money wasn't really a very good basis for a relationship. We had no financial ties; I had a decent salary and was therefore independent, so......and yet, and yet....as I stood on that corner, wreathed in exhaust and grief, my arse full of cum and my heart full of sorrow, I felt.....I felt....obliged to look after the old fart somehow. A decision that would bite me on the bum as it turned out, but then, at that moment, my heart softening, I felt that I couldn't really leave him behind. And darling Sam, a big boy now, was firmly lodged in my heart too, and so...so we all had to go. As a family.

I went in, sober now.

"John," I said. *"I'm moving back to Cornwall. You can come with me if you want. With the pets. But I AM going. I can't be here now."*

"Fuck me!" he said. *"That's come out of nowhere. What brought that on? Did something happen at the funeral?"* If only you knew, I thought, but chose not to enlighten him.

'If you have to ASK........' I thought, but said: *"I just think it's time for a change of scene. It will be nice* (for me) *to be nearer my parents and Gill's back there. You like her, don't you. It will be nice. Back near the sea, the high cliffs...."*

And as I spoke, I knew how right I was. It was like a flower reopening, as I thought about returning to the place I truly belonged.

• • •
146

"So, I'll start looking for jobs, when I get back on Monday. Fancy a pint? Time for last orders..."

We went in to the pub and I got a couple of beers.

"Sorry, I left early. But. You know. What with the pets an' all........!

I knew he wasn't very good round death and dead people or even dying people and I was glad he HAD gone. If he had stayed, Bill wouldn't have fucked me and there would not have been that seminal moment (no pun intent ended) where I knew that it was done. Over. That paradigm shift from sorrow to strength of purpose. Here's Chris saying: *'Stop fuckin mopin' about, you miserable cunt. Get on with it, do something new.'* And with his permission, I was about to.

"Another pint?" I said, sure that even HE wouldn't have a hissy fit, tonight of all nights.

"Go on then. One for the M11......"

Then some *BASTARD* put on Level 42, singing *'It's Over'*; that, coupled with John inadvertently quoting Rod, undid me. The strong beer I was drinking had reactivated the gallons of gin I'd consumed and I fell to pieces, right there, in my local, in front of Alan the butch barman, in front of the quiz team, in front of John. In front of the WHOLE FUCKING BASTARD WORLD.

MY BEST FRIEND WAS DEAD. DEAD. DEAD. DEAD. DEAD.

All these hours and weeks and months of knowing he was dying, watching him turn from man to ghost, watching him choking on his own body fluids as he STILL sought to reassure me, and even apologise, became all too much. I just shattered, broke in to shards of grief. And I wept. And sobbed. And wailed like a lost soul.

I just clung to the bar rail, while everyone stared.

"It's OK. His friend just died."

"Oh, I'm sorry," said Alan. *"Was he young?"*

"'Bout 45."

"Oooh, that's young. What was it?"

"Oh, erm," said John, *"Pneumonia, I think."* and he prised my fingers off the bar rail and began to drag me out of the pub, before, presumably, I could mention

THE WORD, which would, by association, mark *him* out as a poof, a homo, a queer.....like no-one knew, with his Village People moustache, his flappy hands and the fact we lived together in a one bedroom flat right next to the pub......

......dragged me away, sobbing, snotty, gasping for air, crying in the way only a drunk man can cry. In act of gentleness, uncharacteristic, as it would've involved showing feelings, he lay me gently on the bed, and stayed with me until I fell asleep.

I didn't eat for days, went to school, and rehashed old lesson plans as I seemed to be unable to think properly. How could he be dead? He'd ALWAYS been there, guiding, swearing, loving me. Dead? No, not him. Yet he was, and I knew that I was on my own – John was about as much use as a chocolate fireguard, and I seemed to be working on autopilot, running on empty.

"I'm really sorry about your friend," said Sue, resting her hand gently on mine. *"You seem very upset.....maybe....maybe you should get away from here, and all the things that remind you?"*

Before this small act of kindness could undo me, I forced down the lump that was threatening to block my vocal cords and voiced my decision. As Kate Bush once said*: 'Even saying it can really make it happen'* – I said: *"I am. I have already decided. I'm going home."*

"No, I meant away away........."

"That's what I meant too. Not home to the flat; home to HOME. Cornwall. Back home. Where I should never had left and then none of this would have happened. I wouldn't have gone to College, never have met Chris and he would have died and it wouldn't have mattered because I wouldn't have even known him. I can't stay here now, I just can't..." and burst, once more into a spate of uncontrollable weeping.

"For fuck's sake, stop crying, you tart. No wonder you haven't got any friends. You're such a miserable cunt that's why. It's not all about you, you know. And you're FORTY FUCKIN TWO! Grow a pair, get another job and do something useful. Anyway, think how much beer money you'll be saving..."

I heard his voice, and my tears turned to smiles and then to resolve.

I went to staff room and picked up the Times Ed. Supp. and began to search. And, as if he was guiding me, there it was: a job, in a school, in North Cornwall, not far from Truro where Ma and Pa were now living. It was like Fate or

Providence, or maybe just Mr Lucky had returned – and the interviews were still two weeks away.

So.

Phone call; speak to nice lady with Proper Accent, you.

Interview invite.

Train to Cornwall.

Stay at Mum and Dad's. (No mention of anything remotely homosexual or connected to me or my life).

Interview. In purple suit.

Hand shaken and 'welcomed aboard'.

Train back to London.

Resignation from Handsworth.

Leaving party.

Get away with dry humping Sue and fiddling with her lummies. (God, I KNOW!! I have NO idea...)

Start packing......

This was easier said than done. John had to sell his little van and all his Trill and cuttlefish (*LAHVELY! AN ONLY A PAHND!*) about which he was not happy, but, I reasoned we'd have little use for it at the other end so the money would be more useful. And NOT for going to the pub every bloody day, while still working. Pack, man. PACK! Pack up all your horrible tatt, and cheap print of the *'Crying Boy'*, *'The Blue Russian'* bint and *'The Wings of Love'* with the two naked people enfolded in giant swan's wings. Jeez. Am I REALLY gay? I want O'Keefe and Klimt, John Lewis and Libertys, not this old shit! But, it was *quid pro quo*, and I was taking the boy out of Lahndahn.....only fair he should have his stuff I suppose....

Anyway, I worked up till the end of the Spring term, of '88 and, leaving John amidst the chaos of boxes and cat hair, went back to Cornwall and to my Mum and Dad' as my house (£28,000! Bargain!) had still to be finalised. So I moved in with them for what seemed like eternity, though it was in fact only six weeks. In the spare room, me and Sade,

● ● ●

"I still, really love you, love is stronger than pride......"

Over and over, but unsure who I was playing it for......

...struggling to have any conversation that didn't include ANY details of the last twelve years of my life. Mum DID ask about Chris; she knew he'd been ill but had never asked what with, probably guessing and therefore that too was out of bounds. I had taken Chris down to Newquay once during a school holiday, long long ago, and I remember my Mum saying, in a hurried whispered conversation (in the very same bedroom my Dad had caught me sucking Peter off! Lol what irony*!*), *"He's a very nice boy, you know....for one of those. I hope you're being careful?"* (Mother, what ARE you implying??). *"There's this awful new disease going round. I saw it on the telly."* I just told her he'd died and left it at that. Another anonymous passing, cloaked in shame.

Julie was of more interest, (naturally) but I didn't have much news.

Ummmm.....no, I really am NOT going to get back together with her.

Ummmmm......no there really aren't any nice girls (they're not girls, they're women) at my new school. Well, there are, but they're married and / or straight. And anyway, what difference would it make?

Ummmmmm.......hope you won't be lonely in your new house on your own. Who will do the cooking for you? FFS! This is 1988 not 1833. I WILL! ME! USELESS LI'L ME......

I should add that at this point they didn't know about John – and probably just as well. For now. The six weeks passed agonisingly slowly, with Dad ringing the solicitor about eight times a day, implying that he was useless and what was he paying him for...? Yes, dear reader – my Father had agreed to loan me the money for the house purchase – yet something else he would hurl at me for the rest of his life when I did something he didn't agree with. Which was pretty much all the time. And THIS is why I'd decided not to mention John – another Spawn of Satan who went around sodomising everyone, no doubt! Another fully paid up member of the SSU! He certainly wouldn't have agreed to 'promote the homosexual lifestyle' by lending me the money. That's why he thought I was coming on my own. Leaving London and its perversions; leaving the sins of the flesh and returning to Cornwall where, as if by magic, there would be no cock! His boy – no longer a Union member, and now an upstanding pillar of the community and all round good egg. Well, two outa three ain't bad, as Meatloaf once said.

• • •

There was cock aplenty, as I was to discover, but for now, I had my own supply waiting for me back up north of the Tamar; I'm afraid to admit that, really, that was ALL he was – so why may you ask, was I bringing him with me. 'Cuz I luv 'im' wasn't really true. I suppose it was some kind of security – new Job, new house, new social circle...maybe a bit too scary on my own. I don't know, but whatever....

...the house came through, I got the keys, moved out of Uplands Crescent and in to my own house. Mine. The first thing I had ever owned. Well, Barclays bank owned it, but you know what I mean. All it needed now, as I walked through the echoing council house rooms (Cheers Maggie! 'Right To Buy'! Right for me!) was furniture, and my dog. Oh, and John. So, off I went, back to London, back to Walthamstow, back to the tiny flat caked in dog hair and smelling of cat piss, stacked in every corner with John's furniture and I knew that I had made the right decision.

We hired a van, and set off, axles scraping the tarmac, everything we owned, plus the cats, the dogs, all drugged up to the eyeballs, squashed in to every available space and, given that Sam was now the size of a small horse, was no mean feat. Even Freddie had decided it wasn't *'quite nice'* at all and had withdrawn under his wing, fortunately – given the van weighed about 400 tons and therefore our speed was likely to be about 30mph, him shouting *QUITE NICE!* For the next 36hours was not an appealing thought.

However, we were on our way. All regrets packed up along with the boxes of shit I had determined I would gradually lose/break/sell over time until it (and its accompanying smell of animal faeces and bad memories) had gone and been replaced with new, to go with my New Life.

M4.....

M5.....

A30.....

Home.

Sorted! I was free! A proper homosexualist, with a BF, a house, a job and a future. I wasn't going to die 'old and lonely', thank you very much. I had shagged my way round the East End, drunk the barrels dry. I had 'found myself'! I'd gone looking – from Newquay to Hertford, through Blackheath and Deptford, to Leyton, Leytonstone and Walthamstow – not a particularly salubrious journey, but just as surely as other explorers, as surely as Mungo Park had found the Niger and Dr. Livingstone, the Victoria Falls, I had, knowingly or not, found my goal. True, I was currently lumbered with an oaf and several malodorous animals, but I DID have the aforementioned material things AND, more importantly, I had ME and the sense that being a big old poof wasn't a death sentence, an affliction, or something not to be seen or heard in Polite Society. I liked me. I liked my life. I liked men and their willies and was no longer afraid of such a notion.

I thought back to that long-ago pavement, outside of 'Brief Encounter', with dear Chris, Chris the Skinhead, lost and not knowing where I belonged exactly. Which hanky should I have? Which side should I wear it? And I realise, now, that none of that matters. I YAM WHAT I YAM, and if you don't like it, you can go fuck yourself. I'm not in a group, I'm not a 'type' (though I most definitely HAD a type, so it was just as well there WERE types, or I wouldn't have a type to like!), I don't wear any identifiable uniform.....was THIS what is was all about? Blending in? Being Normal? I bloody well hope not! After all the blood, sweat and tears (actually, not blood; substitute that for 'cum') that I'd been through, all the heartache and betrayals and betrayings – I hadn't waded through this amount of shit to come out the other end NORMAL.

Although......

......what was about to happen? I had a wife (read: John), 2.4 kids (read: dogs and cats), a house, a 9-5 (well, 8 – 7.30) job and a mortgage....you don't get much more normal than that. Bugger.

I wanted it to be......I don't know...GLORIOUS! SPARKLY! NOISY AND RAINBOW COLOURED!!! Instead, I was in a van, heading for suburban oblivion, with a load of shit furniture, 5 crapping machines and a man I knew I didn't love.

M4.....

M5.....

A30.....

Roads to Cornwall, the land of my birth, the place my heart resides. And the place that would eventually see me shrink, waste away and become SO small, you wouldn't even know I was there.....

I couldn't decide if I was lucky or not. Probably not, on balance.

We parked up.

There it is, in the middle. The white one.

Now what? Who knew? And if I had, would I have come.....?

'Fings could only get bettah', said Howard Jones, back in '85. How wrong could he be? Although......in the end, he was right.......but not until they'd got worse.

A whole lot worse.

Lightning Source UK Ltd.
Milton Keynes UK
UKOW06f1916210915

259023UK00005B/114/P